QUARTET ENCOUNTERS

RODIN AND OTHER PROSE PIECES

Rilke wrote his monograph on Rodin in 1903. He was 28 and had arrived in Paris the previous year, though for some time he had been familiar with Rodin's work.

Rilke's concept of sculpture as essentially object no longer seems to characterize the work of Rodin. Yet his notion of the work of art as 'thing', in the world but not of it, 'isolated from the spectator as though by a non-conducting vacuum', he projected into the sculpture of Rodin. Rilke saw sculpture as the necessary art for that moment in history, at once object and process, located in everyday reality and imagination's inner world. This monograph is both a homage to Rodin's greatness, and to his colossal influence on the young poet Rilke.

It is published here with Rilke's lecture on Rodin, given in 1907, and several shorter works, including *The Lay of the Love and Death of Cornet Christoph Rilke*.

RAINER MARIA RILKE

Rilke is perhaps the most famous of all twentieth-century European poets. For some months he was Rodin's secretary which placed him in a unique position for understanding not only the sculpture, but also the man himself.

RAINER MARIA RILKE

Rodin and Other Prose Pieces

Translated from the German by
G. CRAIG HOUSTON
With an Introduction by
WILLIAM TUCKER

QUARTET ENCOUNTERS

Quartet Books   London   Melbourne   New York

Published by Quartet Books Limited 1986
A member of the Namara Group
27/29 Goodge Street, London W1P 1FD

Copyright © **Ausgewählte Werke** II, Insel Verlag 1948
Translation copyright © 1954 by The Hogarth Press
Introduction copyright © 1986 by William Tucker

This selection was first published by The Hogarth Press. The present edition contains some additional material on Rodin.

British Library Cataloguing in Publication Data

Rilke, Rainer Maria
Rodin and Other Prose Pieces
1. Rodin, Auguste
I. Title
730'.92'4   NB553.R7

ISBN 0–7043–3495–X

Reproduced, printed and bound in Great Britain
by Nene Litho and Woolnough Bookbinding
both of Irthlingborough, Northants

CONTENTS

	Page
List of Illustrations	vii
Introduction	ix
The Rodin-Book: First Part (Written in Paris, 1902; first published 1903)	1
The Rodin-Book: Second Part (A lecture delivered and published in 1907)	44
Various notes relating to Rodin (1900 and 1902; first published in *Verse und Prosa aus dem Nachlass*, 1929)	72
Description of three sculptures by Rodin (c. 1905)	75
Concerning Landscape (Written early 1902; first published in the *Insel-Almanach* for 1933)	77
Worpswede (Written early in 1902 as the introduction to an illustrated monograph on the Worpswede artists; published in 1903)	82
From the Dream-Book (Written between 1902 and 1907; first published in *Deutsche Arbeit*, 1907/8)	99
An Encounter (Written at Capri in January 1907; first published in the *Wiener Zeitung*, 18 May 1907)	106
An Experience (I) (Written in Spain at the beginning of 1913; first published in the *Insel-Almanach*, 1919)	110
An Experience (II) (Same date and place; first published in *Ausgewählte Werke*, 1938)	112

Note-Book Entry (Written at Ronda, 6
  January 1913; first published in
  Ausgewählte Werke, 1938)   115
Memory (Written September 1914; first
  published in Carl Sieber's *René Rilke*,
  1932)   116
Some Reflections on Dolls (Written early
  in 1914; first published in *Die weissen
  Blätter*, 1913/14)   119
Primal Sound (Written 15 August 1919, at
  Soglio, Graubünden; first published in
  Das Inselschiff, 1919/20)   127
The Young Poet (Written in 1913,
  privately printed at Hamburg in 1931;
  published in the *Insel-Almanach*,
  1939)   133
Concerning the Poet (Written at Duino in
  January 1912; first published in *Verse
  und Prosa aus dem Nachlass*, 1929)   140
The Young Workman's Letter (Written at
  Muzot between 12 and 15 February
  1922; first published 1933)   143
The Lay of the Love and Death of Cornet
  Christoph Rilke (Written in the
  Autumn of 1899 at Schmargendorf,
  Berlin; revised in 1904 and 1906; first
  published in 1906)   155

LIST OF ILLUSTRATIONS

I. Mask of the Man with the Broken Nose (Musée Rodin).
II. The Age of Bronze (Victoria and Albert Museum).
III. St John the Baptist (Victoria and Albert Museum).
IV. The Muse 'La Méditation' (Tate Gallery).
V. Hand (Victoria and Albert Museum).
VI. The Kiss (Tate Gallery).
VII. The Eternal Idol (Musée Rodin).
VIII. Gates of Hell (Musée Rodin).
IX. The Thinker (Musée Rodin).
X. The Danaïd (Musée Rodin).
XI. The Fallen Caryatid Carrying her Stone (Tate Gallery).
XII. Jean-Paul Laurens (Musée Rodin).
XIII. Monument to Victor Hugo (Musée Rodin).
XIV. Monument to Balzac (Musée Rodin).
XV. 'Le Guignon', illustration from *Les Fleurs du Mal*.
XVI. 'La Beauté', illustration from *Les Fleurs du Mal*.

RILKE'S 'RODIN' – AN INTRODUCTION

Lyric poetry in a language we do not speak can never speak to us. The best translation can communicate the experience of the poem itself, in its own words, as effectively as a Polaroid of the Belvedere Torso. J.B. Leishman, who learned German specifically for the lifetime task of translating Rilke's poetry, in the end could demonstrate only the intensity of his belief in Rilke: the intensity of the poetry itself had slipped through his fingers. Lyric poetry being the utmost concentration not only of one individual's experience, but also of the images, thoughts and feelings possible in only one language, the 'translations' of one writer by another of equal stature – as Rilke's own translations of Valéry – are not so much translations as new poems.

Rilke wrote many prose works and letters which do not present the same difficulty of access to the English reader, but then neither do they offer the same focusing of experience, or anything near to it; with one exception, and that is the book on Rodin. For here the images belong to the reader of no one language ('the language of this art was the body', as Rilke wrote), but to everyone with the slightest interest in art: even that might not be necessary for the casual reader who, carried by the strong current of the writing far into the book, could hardly finish it without the desire to explore its subject at first hand. But it is not a work of art criticism, or art history, much less an artist's biography ('his life is one of those which cannot be told . . . it must have had a childhood . . . And perhaps it has this childhood still' . . . the words 'maybe' and 'perhaps' are frequent in the early pages); because this is not so much a book about the sculptor and sculpture, as about the artist and his art, the poet and his poetry. Rodin's work emerges from these pages simultaneously as the achievement of the old artist, and the dream and goal of the young poet. Through the effort to understand what Rodin had done, Rilke came to understand what he had to do.

Toward the end of his life, Rilke wrote in reply to some

questions about his own biography: 'When I moved to Paris in 1902, Richard Muther had suggested that I write about Rodin; for his work (though even then of plastic art little, according to its true value, had as yet become significant to me) I seemed prepared, inasmuch as my wife has the right to consider herself a pupil of Rodin's; through her ... I had become more capable of comprehending works of art from the standpoint of *form* and seemed a trace more safeguarded against chance overpowerings by mere relations of content, which act upon the unprepared person, even through the most inadequate handling of form, if they in any way touch him ...' But the Rodin book is scarcely formal criticism, even formal description: for 'form' we should perhaps read 'essence' or 'core' – and this not a static universal arrived at after the fact, but a process, a dynamic principle of becoming identified in the workshop rather than the museum. 'His art was not based upon any great idea, but upon the conscientious realization of something small, upon something capable of achievement, upon a matter of technique.'

The young Rilke, already celebrated as the author of the accomplished but dubious *The Lay of the Love and Death of Cornet Christoph Rilke*, approached Rodin as he had earlier (and disastrously) approached Tolstoy, as an older artist of enormous reputation, whose example might give him a firmer hold on his own amazing but wayward lyric gift; he needed a father in art to replace the father who he felt had failed him in life. The need was powerful, but it was internal – the motor of a lifelong spiritual quest that was to take him past Rodin, then past Cézanne, toward the continuously receding horizon of the fundamental questions: 'Who if I screamed would hear me among the angels?' and 'Are we perhaps *here* to say: House, Bridge, Fountain, Door, Jug . . .?'

And if Rilke, in an external sense, did not need the commission to write the Rodin book, Rodin in 1902 at the height of his fame – he was indeed the best known artist in the world at that time – certainly did not need Rilke in particular to add to his glory. The tone of uncritical admiration, almost worship, that pervades the text no doubt satisfied its subject, but for us it is its least happy aspect. The core of the book is in fact Rilke's fresh and original perception of the work, fuelled no doubt by conversation with the artist, but founded in the intuition of the most sensitive amateur, the very opposite of the professional critic or publicist. The book in which these perceptions are embodied survived the collapse of Rodin's reputation after his death, as it has remained the most

INTRODUCTION

profound appreciation during the Rodin revival of the last three decades. Paradoxically Rilke, in identifying with Rodin, found his own centre by pointing to Rodin's. The book endured because of a wholeness and sense of purpose within Rilke's work, that some historical distance has shown to be absent from Rodin's œuvre, elements of which will always be problematic even to the most devoted admirers of a century later.

The reasons for these flaws lie partly in the historical predicament of the ambitious sculptor (as opposed to the painter) in nineteenth-century France, and partly in Rodin's own complex personality. The sculptor needed public commissions and state patronage in order to survive as an artist, and Rodin was driven by nature to confront, shock, charm or amaze a public – he needed the response of an audience as much as Dickens or Wagner. It was this charged relation with the audience – an audience of widely differing expectations – that makes the work so uneven in clarity and aspiration. Rodin made the finest Realist sculptures of the nineteenth century – the studies for the *Burghers of Calais* and the *Balzac* – and the finest Romantic sculptures – the Balzac monument, many of the figures from the *Gates of Hell*; but they were made long after Delacroix and Courbet, and the urgency of the historic moment had passed. He belonged by birth to the generation of the Impressionists, but his prolonged craft apprenticeship had kept him separate from their common enterprise. Yet Rilke rightly perceived that Rodin's central task was to liberate sculpture, as the Impressionists had liberated painting, but internally, in a way that was appropriate to sculpture alone: '... with regard to the painter at least came the understanding and the belief that an artistic whole need not necessarily coincide with the complete thing ... in the art of sculpture also it is left to the artist to make out of many things one thing, and from the smallest part of a thing an entirety.' The first impression Rilke described to his wife of Rodin's studio at Meudon in 1902 was of 'acres of fragments ... nudes the size of my hand and bigger, but only bits, scarcely one of them whole: often only a piece of arm, a piece of leg, just as they go together and the portion of the body that belongs with them ... and yet the closer you look the deeper you feel all would be less complete if the separate bodies were complete. Each of these fragments is of such a peculiarly striking unity, so possible by itself, so little in need of completion that you forget they are only parts and often parts of different bodies which cling so passionately to one another ...'

He wrote a few days later of a conversation with the sculptor, who 'always came back to things, to the life of these things – de regarder une pierre, la torse d'une femme . . . and always, again and again, to work. Ever since the physical, the really heavy work of the craftsman has been regarded as something inferior, he said, work has ceased altogether. I know five, six, people in Paris who really work, perhaps a few more. There in the schools, what they do year in and year out – they "make compositions". In this way they learn absolutely nothing of the nature of things . . . You see, for him there is *only* the *modelé* . . . on all things, on all bodies, he detaches it from them and after he has learned it from them he makes of it an independent entity, that is, a work of sculpture.'

To be sure, Rilke in his book spends time on the Romantic and Realist Rodin – but the thought of the book revolves around these first impressions; the wholeness of the fragment, the thing, work, modelling, surface – these are not separate ideas, but aspects of the same idea. So, early in the text: 'Work . . . and you will have the grace of great things' and '[sculpture] was something which could exist for its own sake alone, and it was well to give it absolutely the character of an object round which one could pass and which could be observed from all sides.' Of the *Mask of the Man with the Broken Nose*: 'There was no symmetry in the planes of this face, no repetition, no part empty, uncommunicative or neutral . . . its beauty . . . comes . . . from the feeling that all these factors of disturbance come to rest within the thing itself.' Of the body of 'The Man of Early Times' (*The Age of Bronze*), 'each part was a mouth uttering . . . in its own manner.' And in the concluding paragraph: 'Some day men will understand what it was that made this great artist so great, the fact, namely, that he was a worker who desired nothing but to participate with all his powers in the humble and difficult existence of his medium.'

These insights remind us that Rilke was of the same generation as Brancusi and the other young sculptors attracted to Paris by Rodin's reputation in the early years of the century, and who were soon to begin the task of reducing his sprawling achievement to the essentials of form and construction. They were well aware of their debt. Many years later Brancusi wrote: 'In the nineteenth century the position of sculpture was one of despair. Then Rodin appeared and succeeded in transforming everything. Thanks to him, man became once more the measure, the model from which the statue springs. Thanks to him too, sculpture became human again both in its dimensions and its spiritual content.'

INTRODUCTION

Rilke's real understanding of Rodin's art is coupled with the image of the sculptor himself as the solitary sage, the philosopher-craftsman. This image belongs more to fiction than to history: but it gives the book the wholeness of a myth that would be perfectly convincing had Rodin been the most indifferent sculptor, or indeed had no more existed than Balzac's Frenhofer.

William Tucker

Note

This introduction was written primarily in regard to Rilke's original (1903) essay on Rodin, which was available for many years by itself in an English translation. It was a well-worn copy of this slim volume that found its way into my hands as a student in the late fifties, and fired an enthusiasm for the art of sculpture (if not at that time for the art of Rodin) that I later discovered was the common experience of many artists on their first encounter with this inspiring text. It was, and I hope still is, a kind of secret gospel for sculptors, affirming a vision of the art that transcends differences of style, subject and material.

Some years afterward, when I became interested in Rilke himself as a writer, I came across the 1907 'Lecture'. It is a more conscious and considered work, essentially an amplification of elements from the earlier text. This is especially true of the beautiful opening section of 'Things', where we see Rilke developing a theme learned from Rodin, which he had already made his own and which was to be at the core of his mature poetry (the 'New Poems' were published in 1908). The body of the lecture is a portrait of the sculptor based plainly on a closer acquaintanceship than that of established artist and young admirer. In fact a real friendship had developed between the two men, and Rodin offered to help Rilke financially by employing him as a secretary. The project did not work out well, but Rilke's respect for the older man as an artist was not diminished.

The notes and fragments here collected with the essay and the lecture, date from 1900, two years before Rilke first met Rodin, to 1919, two years after Rodin's death: we can watch the unfolding of Rilke's appreciation of sculpture, of his relationship with Rodin, and of his self-understanding as a writer, for whom the sculptor and his *métier* had been so fruitful a model.

W.T.

Editor's Note
There are small differences between the titles of some works referred to in the text and in the Introduction. Those in the Introduction are the titles in current usage.

The Rodin-Book

FIRST PART
(1903)

SECOND PART
(1907)

Writers operate through words,
Sculptors through deeds.
>
> POMPONIUS GAURICUS,
> *De Sculptura* (*c. 1504*)

The hero is he who is immovably centred.
>
> EMERSON

FIRST PART

RODIN was solitary before he became famous. And Fame, when it came, made him if anything still more solitary. For Fame, after all, is but the sum of all the misunderstandings which gather about a new name.

There are a great many about Rodin and it would be a long and difficult task to elucidate them. Nor is it necessary. They surround the name, not the work which has far outgrown the sounding greatness of the name and is now nameless, as a plain is nameless or an ocean, the name of which is found only on maps, in books or in the mouths of men, but which, in reality, is only vastness, movement, and depth.

The work of which we are to speak here has been growing for years and grows every day like a forest, losing no hour of time. Passing amongst its thousand manifestations, one is overwhelmed by the wealth of the discoveries and inventions it embraces, and instinctively one looks for the two hands from which this world has come forth. One thinks of the smallness of human hands, of how soon they weary and of how little time is granted to their activity. And one longs to behold these hands which have lived the life of a hundred hands, of a nation of hands, that rose before daybreak to set out on the long pathway of this work. One asks about the owner of these hands. Who is this man?

He is an old man. And his life is one of those which cannot be told. A life which has had a beginning and which advances, advances far into a great age, and to us it seems as if it had been lived many hundreds of years since. We know nothing of it. It must have had a childhood of some kind, a childhood of poverty, dark, groping, and uncertain. And perhaps it has this childhood still, for—as St. Augustine once said—whither should it have gone? Perhaps it still has all its past hours, hours of expectancy and hours of loneliness, hours of despair and the long hours of distress; it is a life in which nothing has been lost or forgotten, a life which as it passed was stored up. Perhaps, we cannot tell. But we believe that only from such a life could the wealth and abundance of this activity proceed, that only such a life, in which everything is present and alive and nothing past, can remain young and strong, rising with constantly renewed inspiration to works which are sublime. The time may come when the history of this life will be invented, its ramifications, its episodes, its details. They will have to be invented. There will be the story of a child who often forgot to eat, because it seemed to him much more important to carve things in common wood with a blunt knife, and from the days of his boyhood will be dated some episode containing a promise of future greatness, one of those prophecies after the event which make so touching an appeal to the simple. It may quite well be the words which some monk is said to have addressed almost five hundred years ago to the young Michel Colombe, these words: "Travaille, petit, regarde tout ton saoul et le clocher à jour de Saint-Pol, et les belles œuvres des compaignons, regarde, aime le bon Dieu, et tu auras la grâce des grandes choses." "And you will have the grace of great things." Perhaps it was thus, but in tones infinitely softer than those of monkish mouth, that some hidden feeling spoke to the youth at one of the crossroads in the days of his first beginnings. For that was what he sought: the grace of great things. There was the Louvre with its many luminous objects of the antique, suggestive of southern skies and the proximity of the sea, and behind these rose other, heavy things in stone, lasting from incredibly distant civilizations into ages which were still to come. There were stones asleep, and one felt that they would awaken at some Judgment Day, stones which had nothing mortal about them, and others embodying a movement, a gesture, which had retained such freshness that it seemed to be preserved here only until some passing child should receive it one day as a gift. And not only in the famous works of art and in those visible from afar did this quality of life exist; the unnoticed, the small, the nameless, and superfluous were no less filled with this deep inner vitality, with the rich and amazing restlessness of life. Even the tranquillity, where there was tranquillity, was composed of hundreds upon hundreds of moments of motion keeping each other in equilibrium. There were small figures, particularly beasts, moving, stretching or crouching, and even when a bird was at rest one knew at once that it was a bird, there went forth from it a sky which remained about it, distance lay folded on each of its feathers, one could spread it out and make it vast. And it was the same with the animals standing or lying on the cathedrals or crouching under the consoles, stunted and crumpled up and too inert to bear the weight. There were dogs and squirrels, woodpeckers and lizards, tortoises, rats, and snakes. At least one of each kind. These creatures appeared to have been captured out in the woods and on the highways, and the constraint of living among tendrils, flowers, and leaves of stone must have changed them slowly into what they now were and would henceforth remain. But one also came across creatures born in their stone surroundings, who had no recollection of any other existence. From the beginning they were entirely native in this perpendicular, towering, steeply rising world. Consorting with their fanatic leanness were figures of skeletons in the pointed-arch style, their mouths opened wide and shouting, like those who are deaf, for the proximity of the bells had destroyed their hearing. They supported no weight, but stretched themselves, thus helping the stones to soar upward. Some, like birds, crouched aloft on the balustrades, as though their flight were not yet finished and they were but resting a century or two to gaze down upon the growing town. Others, descended from dogs, thrust themselves out horizontally from the edge of the spouting into the air, ready to emit, from jaws swollen in the effort, the rains' water. All of them, transformed and modified, had yet lost nothing of their vitality, on the contrary, they lived more vigorously, more violently, lived for all time the passionate and impetuous life of the age which gave them birth.

And anyone seeing this imagery felt it was not born of any mood, nor of any playful desire to find new, unheard-of forms. Necessity had created it. Fearful of the invisible tribunals of an oppressive faith, men had sought refuge in these visible forms, had escaped from the unknown to this concrete embodiment. Still seeking reality in God, men showed their piety, not any longer by inventing images for Him and seeking to picture the All-too-distant-one, but by bringing into His house, laying in His hand and on His heart all the fear and poverty, all the timidity and the gestures of the humble. This was a better way than by painting, for painting was also an illusion, a beautiful and skilful deception; they desired something more real, something simple. Thus there came about the strange sculpture of the cathedrals, this sacred procession of the heavy-laden and the beasts.

And looking from the plastic art of the Middle Ages back to the antique, and again beyond the antique to the beginning of eras whose age cannot be reckoned, did it not seem that at every hopeful or disquieting turning-point of history the human soul had ever and again demanded this art which gives more than word and picture, more than similitude and appearance, this simple becoming-concrete of its longings or its apprehensions? Finally, in the Renaissance, there arose a great plastic art; at that period when life was renewed, when the mystery of the human countenance was discovered, when gesture in all its greatness developed.

And now? Was not this again an age demanding the same mode of expression, the same strong and penetrative interpretation of all in it which defied utterance, which was confused and enigmatic? The arts had in some way become renewed, filled and animated by eager expectation; perhaps it was just this plastic art, still hesitating in the shadow of a great past, which was destined to find that which the sister arts were feeling for gropingly and with a great desire. It surely possessed the power to bring help to an age tormented by conflicts which lay, almost without exception, in the realm of the invisible. The language of this art was the body. And when had this body last been seen? Layer upon layer of clothing had been laid upon it like constantly renewed varnish, but beneath these protecting incrustations the living soul, breathlessly at work upon the human face, had transformed the body too. It had become a different body. If it were now uncovered, it would probably reveal a thousand forms of expression for all that was new and nameless in its development, and for all those ancient secrets which, emerging from the Unconscious, like strange river gods, lift their dripping heads from out the wild current of the blood. And this body could not but be as beautiful as that of the Greeks. It must possess even greater beauty. Two thousand years more of Life had held it between its hands, had wrought upon it, caught its secrets and had not ceased to work upon it day and night. Painting had dreamt of this body, had adorned it with radiance and steeped it in twilight, had surrounded it with delicacy and charm of every kind, had felt its texture as one feels the petal of a flower, had been borne along by it as by a wave—but in plastic art, to which it properly belonged, it was as yet unknown.

Here was a task great as the world itself. And he who stood facing it was a man unknown, whose hands sought blindly for bread. He stood alone, and had he been only a dreamer he might have dreamt a dream deep and beautiful, which none would have understood, one of those long, long dreams in the dreaming of which life passes like a day. But this young man, employed in the factory at Sèvres, was a dreamer whose dream went to his hands and he began forthwith to achieve its realization. He felt where he must begin; a calmness in him showed him the true way. At this point is revealed that deep agreement with Nature, which is characteristic of Rodin and which has been described so well by the poet Georges Rodenbach, who calls him simply "an elemental force". And, indeed, there is in Rodin a deep patience which makes him almost anonymous, a quiet, wise forbearance, something of the great patience and kindness of Nature herself, who, beginning with some negligible quantity, traverses silently and seriously the long pathway to abundance. Neither did Rodin presume to create trees full-grown. He began with the seed, below the surface as it were. And this seed grew downwards, struck many roots downwards and anchored firmly, before the first small shoot rose upward. This meant time and yet more time. "It does not do to hurry," said Rodin to the few friends about him, who urged him forward.

Then the war [1] came and Rodin went to Brussels to do the work which each day brought with it. He did some figures on private houses and several of the groups on the Exchange Buildings and carved the four large corner figures of the monument to Burgomaster Loos in the park of Anvers. Commissions which he carried out conscientiously, without any expression of his own growing personality. His own development went on simultaneously, uneasily in the cramped intervals of the day and in evening hours, spaciously in the solitary stillness of the night; and this division of his energies he had to suffer for many years. But he had the strength of those for whom some great work is waiting, the silent endurance of those whom the world needs.

Whilst at work upon the Brussels Exchange, he must have felt that buildings no longer attracted sculpture to them, as did the old cathedrals, those great magnets of the plastic art of a bygone age. The piece of sculpture was a thing standing apart as the picture was apart, the easel-picture, but, unlike the latter, it did not need even a wall. Nor even a roof. It was something which could exist for its own sake alone, and it was well to give it absolutely the character of an object round which one could pass and which could be observed from all sides. And yet, it must in some way be distinguished from other things, ordinary things, which anyone may lay hold of. It must be made, by some means, untouchable, sacrosanct, separated from the influence of accident or time, in the midst of which it appears solitary and strange, like the face of some visionary. It must have its own assured place, uninfluenced by arbitrary considerations, and it must be made part of the calm permanence of space and its great laws. It must be fitted into the surrounding air as into a niche and thus be given a security, a stability, a sublimity due to its simple existence and not to its significance.

Rodin knew that the first indispensable factor was an un-

[1] The Franco-Prussian war, 1870 (*Translator's Note*).

erring knowledge of the human body. Slowly, exploringly he had moved from within outwards to its surface, and now a hand from without stretched forward and measured and limited this surface as exactly from without as from within. The further he advanced upon this untrodden way, the further was accident left behind, one law leading him on to another. And ultimately it was this surface which became the subject of his study. It consisted of innumerable effects of light falling upon the object, and it appeared that each of these effects was different and each remarkable. At one place the light seemed to be absorbed, at another to give a lingering greeting, at a third to pass coldly by; and there was no end to such surfaces and no surface where some effect did not take place. No part was blank.

It was at this point that Rodin discovered the fundamental element of his art, as it were, the cell of his world. And this was the plane, the exactly defined plane, of varying size and emphasis, from which all else must be made. From this time onward it was the subject of his art, the object of all his efforts, of his vigilance and his endurance. His art was not based upon any great idea, but upon the conscientious realization of something small, upon something capable of achievement, upon a matter of technique. There was no arrogance in him. He devoted himself to this insignificant and difficult aspect of beauty which he could survey, command and judge. The other, the greater beauty, must come when all was ready for it, as animals come to drink when night holds sway and the forest is free of strangers.

With this discovery began Rodin's own peculiar work. All the traditional conceptions of plastic art now lost their meaning for him. Pose, group, composition, none of these things any longer existed. Only an endless variety of living surfaces, only life; and the mode of expression which he had evolved for himself was immediately concerned with that life. It was henceforth a question of making Life and all its fullness obey his purpose. Rodin seized upon Life as he saw it everywhere about him. He laid hold of its slightest manifestations, he observed it, he sought it out. He lay in wait for it at moments of transition, of hesitation, he overtook it in flight, and everywhere he found it equally great, powerful and enthralling. No part of the body was insignificant or negligible, every part was alive. Life showing in the face, full of reference to time and as easily read as on a dial, was, when seen in the body, less concentrated, greater, more mysterious and eternal. There it wore no disguise. Where it felt indifference, it showed indifference, and in the proud it was proud; leaving the stage of the face, it let fall its mask and revealed itself as it appeared behind the coulisses of clothing. There he found the Life of his own times, as he had found that of the Middle Ages in the architecture of the cathedrals, gathered round a mysterious darkness, held together by an organism to which it was adapted and which it served. Man had become a temple, there were thousands upon thousands of such temples, all of which were alive and no two alike. But the thing was to show that they were all the temples of one God.

For years on end Rodin followed where this Life led him, a humble learner conscious of his own immaturity. His efforts remained unknown, for he had no confidants and but few friends. Sheltered behind the industry which sustained him, his work grew, biding its time. He read much. In the streets of Brussels he was always seen with a book in his hand, a book which was perchance but a cover for his preoccupation with himself and with the tremendous task before him. As in the case of all men of action, the feeling that he had before him a piece of work of indefinite duration acted as an incentive, as something that heightened and concentrated his powers. And when beset by doubts and uncertainties, by the great impatience of conscious immaturity, by the fear of an early death or by the threatened lack of daily necessities, he met these things with a quiet, resolute resistance, a defiance, a strength, a confidence, all the unfurled flags of a great victory. Perhaps, at such times, it was the past which took sides with him, the voice of the cathedrals, that voice which he so unwearily sought out. And books too came to his aid. He read Dante's Divine Comedy for the first time. It was a revelation. With his own eyes he beheld the suffering bodies of another generation, saw, across the intervening days, a century stripped of its covering, saw the great and unforgettable judgment pronounced by a poet upon his own age. There he found pictures proving him to be right, and when he read of the weeping feet of Nicolas the Third, he found that he already knew there could be weeping feet, that there is a weeping of the whole body, of the whole person, and that every pore can bring forth tears. And from Dante he passed to Baudelaire. Here was no tribunal of judgment, no poet mounting to Heaven by ghostly guidance, but a mortal, one of the suffering, lifting up his voice and holding it aloft above the heads of his fellows as if to save them from destruction. And in this poetry there were passages standing out from the rest, not written but, as it seemed, moulded, words and groups of words which had been melted in the burning hands of the poet, lines which felt like reliefs to the touch and sonnets bearing the weight of a troubled thought like columns supporting confusedly-wrought capitals. He felt dimly that this art, stopping abruptly, had stumbled on the beginnings of another, for which it had longed; he felt in Baudelaire one of his own predecessors, an artist who had refused to be led astray by faces, and who sought bodies in which life was greater, more relentless, more restless.

From this time onward these two poets were never far from him, his thoughts reached out beyond them and came back to them. In that preparatory and formative period of his art, when the life of which it was learning was nameless and without meaning, Rodin's thoughts explored the works of the poets and found in them a past. When, later, as a creative artist, he reverted to these spheres of thought, the figures of the poets rose before him in sorrowful reality, like memories coming forth from his own experience, and passed into his work as into their true home.

Finally, after years of solitary work, he decided to make his appearance with one of his works. It was a question put to the public. The public answered in the negative. And Rodin retired within himself again for thirteen years. These were the years during which, still unknown, he ripened into maturity and gained complete mastery over his own medium, working, thinking, experimenting unceasingly, indifferent to a generation which was indifferent to him. Perhaps it was this circumstance of complete development in undisturbed peace to which he owed his tremendous confidence at a later period, when his work had become the object of strife and enmity. When others began to doubt him, he had no longer any doubt of himself. That all lay behind him. His destiny no longer depended upon the approval and the judgment of the multitude, it had already been decided when others imagined they could still destroy it by ridicule and hostility. During this period of development he was undisturbed by any voice from without. There reached him neither praise to mislead him nor blame to confuse him. Like Parzival, his work was cradled in purity, alone with itself and with great eternal Nature. His work alone spoke to him. It spoke to him in the morning when he awoke, and in the evening it reverberated in his hands long after he had laid it aside, like music in an instrument which one has ceased to play. His work was invincible because it came into the world mature; not in a state of development, seeking its justification, but as a triumphant, existing reality which must be reckoned with. Like a king who, hearing that a city is to be built within his realm, considers whether it were well to grant the privilege or not, hesitates, and finally proceeds to view the site; he comes to the place and behold! he finds a great and mighty city already complete, standing as if from all eternity, with walls and towers and gateways: in like manner did the public come to Rodin's work at his summons and found it complete.

The limits of the period in which he attained to maturity are marked by two works. The beginning by the *Man with the Broken Nose*, and the end by the figure of the young man, called by Rodin the *Man of Early Times*. The *Homme au nez cassé* was rejected by the Salon in 1864. The reason is clear, for in this work Rodin's manner is felt to have reached maturity, to be fully developed and confident of itself; with the complete lack of circumspection of a great confession, it contradicted all standards of academic beauty then recognized. In vain had Rude given to his Goddess of Revolt on the triumphal arch in the Place de l'Etoile her wild gesture and wide-mouthed cry; in vain had Barye created his lithe animals; Carpeaux' *Dance* had only been the subject of scorn until familiarity had, finally, deprived it of the power to excite attention. Nothing had changed. The plastic art of the time was still that of the model, the pose, and the allegory; that simple, facile, and effortless *métier* which consists of the more or less skilful repetition of certain approved movements. In such a milieu the head of the *Man with the Broken Nose* might well have aroused the storm which, however, did not break until the appearance of the later works. It may be that, being the work of an unknown artist, it was scarcely looked at when rejected.

We can feel what it was that led Rodin to form this head, the head of an ageing and ugly man, whose broken nose only tends to accentuate the tormented expression of the face; it was the immense concentration of life in these features; the fact that there was no symmetry in the planes of this face, no repetition, no part empty, uncommunicative or neutral. Life had not simply touched this face, it had wrought it through and through, like some inexorable hand thrusting it into destiny and holding it there as in the rush of swirling, cleansing waters. Taking it in one's hands, and causing it to revolve slowly, one is amazed by the ever-changing profiles, not one of which is accidental, uncertain or indefinite. Not a line, not a join, not a contour in this head but had been seen by Rodin and executed with intention. One seems to feel that some of these furrows must have appeared earlier, others later, that different deep-cut marks across the features were separated by years of time and trouble; one knows beyond question that some of the marks on this face were inscribed slowly, almost hesitatingly, that others were at first lightly traced, then firmly drawn in by some recurring habit or thought, and one recognizes the sharp incisions which must have come in a night, as if cut by the beak of a bird, in the weary brow of one whom sleep evades. Only with an effort does one recollect that all this is contained within the space of a face, so great and nameless is the life issuing from this work.

Putting down the mask, one has the sensation of standing on some high tower and looking down upon a rugged landscape, over whose devious ways many peoples have passed. And, taking it up again, one has in one's hands something which must be called beautiful on account of its perfection. But its beauty is not entirely due to its incomparable perfection. It comes from the feeling of equilibrium, of balance between all these living surfaces, from the feeling that all these factors of disturbance come to rest within the thing itself. One's immediate sensation, on feeling the many-voiced torment of this face, is that it utters no accusation. It makes no appeal to the world; it seems to carry within itself its own justice, the reconciliation of all its contradictions and a patience great enough for all its burdens.

When Rodin made this mask he had a man sitting motionless before him with unmoved countenance. But it was the countenance of a living person, and as he studied it, behold, it was full of movement, full of restlessness and the rhythm of waves. There was movement in the direction of the lines, movement in the incline of the planes, the shadows moved as if in sleep and the light seemed to pass softly over the brow. There was, then, no such thing as calm, not even in death; for in decay, which is also movement, even what was dead was still subordinated to life. In Nature there was only movement; and an art that wished to give a conscientious and credible interpretation of life, might not take for its ideal a calm which was non-existent. In reality, classic art knew nothing of such an ideal. One had only to think of the *Victory*. That piece of sculpture gives not merely the movement of a beautiful maiden going forth to meet her lover, it is also an immortal representation of the wind of Greece and of its sweeping glory. Even the stones of earlier civilizations were not without movement. In the restrained, hieratic gestures of ancient religions the restlessness of living surfaces was contained like water within the walls of a vessel. Through taciturn gods in sitting posture there passed currents, and in those standing there was a movement like that of a fountain rising from the marble and returning to it, filling it with many ripples. Movement was not contrary to the spirit of sculpture (that is, to the essence of the thing); only such movement as is incomplete, as is not balanced by other movement, such movement as passes beyond the object itself. The plastic object is comparable to those cities of ancient times whose life was passed entirely within their walls; this does not mean that the citizens held their breath, nor did it cramp their life. But nothing passed beyond the limits of the circle enclosing them, nothing lay on the far side, nothing suggested a world outside, no hopes lay open towards the beyond. However great the movement in a piece of sculpture, whether it comes from infinite distances or from the depths of the heavens, it must return to the marble, the vast circle must be closed, that circle of solitude within which a work of art exists. This was the unwritten law alive in the sculpture of the past. Rodin recognized it. This distinguishing characteristic of things, complete self-absorption, was what gave to plastic art its calm; it must have no desire nor expectation beyond itself, nor bear any reference to what lies beyond, nor be aware of anything outside itself. Its surroundings must be found within it. It was the sculptor Leonardo who gave this quality of unapproachability to the Gioconda, this movement withinwards, this inward gaze which ignores the beholder. Probably his Francesco Sforza had it too, this expression of movement which returns, like some proud ambassador after the fulfilment of his purpose, to the country which has sent him forth.

In the long years which passed between the creation of the mask of the *Man with the Broken Nose* and the figure of the *Man of Early Times* many silent developments took place within Rodin. New associations linked him more closely with the past of his art. That past and its greatness, under which others had laboured as under some heavy burden, lent wings to him, bearing him aloft. For if, at this period, he ever received encouragement and confirmation of his aim and of his quest, it came from the works of the ancients and from out the soft darkness of the cathedrals. Men did not speak to him. Stones spoke.

The *Man with the Broken Nose* had shown Rodin's understanding of the human face, the *Man of Early Times* demonstrated his complete mastery of the human body. "Souverain tailleur d'ymaiges", this title used by the masters of the Middle Ages when, untouched by envy, they appraised each other's worth, was his by right. Here was a life-sized nude figure showing life which was not only equally great in every part but which was, as it seemed, everywhere endowed with the same sublimity of expression. What was expressed in the face, the pain and effort of awakening together with the desire for this awakening, was written on the least part of the body; each part was a mouth uttering it in its own manner. The most searching eye could not discover in this figure any place less alive, less definite, less expressive than another. Strength from the depths of the earth seemed to rise into the veins of this man. He was like the silhouette of a tree with the storms of March still before it, fearful because the summer's fruit and fullness lives no longer in its roots but is already rising slowly, is already in the trunk about which the great winds will blow.

The figure is significant from another point of view. It marks the birth of gesture in Rodin's work. Gesture, which grew and developed gradually to such proportions and power, is here seen emerging like the waters of a spring, and flowing gently over this whole body. It awoke in the darkness of primeval times and seems, as it grows, to flow through the spaciousness of his work as through the ages, passing far beyond us to those who are yet to come. Tentatively it appears in the raised arms, arms still so heavy that the hand of one comes to rest on the crown of the head. But movement has cast off sleep and is gathering force; right on the top, on the apex of the brain where there is solitude, it prepares for its task, the task of centuries, limitless and without end. And in the right foot the first step waits.

One might describe this movement by saying that it rests enclosed in a tight bud. Let thought be set on fire, let the will be swept by tempest, and it will open. And we have that *John* with the eloquent, agitated arms, with the great stride of one who feels another coming after him. This man's body is not untested: the fires of the desert have scorched him, hunger has racked him, thirst of every kind has tried him. He has come through all and is hardened. The lean, ascetic body is like a wooden handle in which is set the wide fork of his stride. He advances, advances as though all the wide spaces of the world were within him, as if he were apportioning them with his stride. He advances. His arms express it, his fingers are widespread, seeming to make the sign of striding forward in the air. This *John* is the first pedestrian figure in Rodin's work. Many follow. There are the *Burghers of Calais*, setting out on their grievous journey, and all his walking figures seem to be but a preparation for the great, challenging step of Balzac.

But the act of standing also develops, it withdraws within itself, curling up like burning paper, it becomes stronger, more concentrated, more vital. As in the figure of Eve,[1] designed originally to stand above the *Gate of Hell*. The head is sunk deep in the shadow of the arms, and these are drawn across the breast as in a figure shivering with cold. The back is rounded, the neck almost horizontal, she stands leaning forward as if to listen to her own body, in which an unknown future begins to stir. It is as if the force of gravity in this future were affecting the woman through her senses and drawing her away from the distractions of life down into the deep, humble service of motherhood.

Rodin reverted again and again in his figures to this turning-inward-upon-oneself, this tense listening to inner depths; we have it in the marvellous figure which he called *La Méditation*, in the unforgettable *Voix intérieure*, the softest voice of Victor Hugo's songs, which forms part of the monument to the poet, standing almost hidden by the Voice of Anger. Never before has human body been so concentrated about itself, been made by its own spirit to bend so, and yet been so upheld by the elastic power of its own blood. The neck stretches slightly upwards, as it rises from the body bent downwards and sideways, and holds the listening head above the distant sounds of life's

[1] In the Tate Gallery (*Translator's Note*).

imult. This is so strikingly and grandly conceived that one can recall no more affecting or significant attitude. The arms are noticeably absent. Rodin felt them in this instance to be too easy a solution of his problem, to be something extraneous to the body, which sought to be its own concealment, without external aid. One recalls Duse, how in one of D'Annunzio's plays, when left bitterly alone, she attempts to give an armless embrace, to hold without hands. This scene, in which her body learns a caress far beyond its natural scope, belongs to the unforgettable moments of her acting. It conveyed the impression that arms were a superfluous adornment, something for the rich and self-indulgent, something which those in the pursuit of poverty could easily cast aside. She looked in that moment not like a person lacking something important; but rather like someone who has given away his cup that he may drink from the stream itself, like someone who is naked and a little helpless in his absolute nakedness. The same effect is produced by the armless statues of Rodin; nothing essential is lacking. We stand before them as before something whole and complete, which allows of no addition. The feeling of incompleteness does not come from the mere aspect of a thing, but is due to elaborate reflexion, to petty pedantry, which says that where there is a body there must be arms, that a body without arms can, in no instance, be complete. Not long ago the same criticism was levelled against the trees of the Impressionists, cut off as they are by the edge of the picture; we very soon became accustomed to such an effect, learning to see and understand, in the case of the painter at any rate, that an artistic whole must not necessarily be identical with the usual thing-whole, that, independent of it, there arise within the picture itself new unities, new associations, relationships and adjustments. It is the same in sculpture. The artist has the right to make one thing out of many and a world out of the smallest part of a thing. Rodin has made hands, independent, small hands which, without forming part of a body, are yet alive. Hands rising upright, angry and irritated, hands whose five bristling fingers seem to bark like the five throats of a Cerberus. Hands in motion, sleeping hands and hands in the act of awaking; criminal hands weighted by heredity, hands that are tired and have lost all desire, lying like some sick beast crouched in a corner, knowing none can help them. But hands are a complicated organism, a delta in which much life from distant sources flows together and is poured into the great stream of action. Hands have a history of their own, they have, indeed, their own civilization, their special beauty; we concede to them the right to have their own development, their own wishes, feelings, moods and favourite occupations.

But, thanks to his self-imposed training, Rodin knows that the body consists of so many stages for the display of life, of such life as in any and every part can be individual and great, and he has the power to bestow on any part of the vast, vibrating surface of the body the independence and completeness of a whole. And, as the human body is for Rodin a whole only so long as all its limbs and powers respond to one common movement (internal or external), so, on the other hand, do parts of different bodies, brought together by inner necessity, become for him a single organism. A hand laid on the shoulder or limb of another body is no longer part of the body to which it properly belongs: something new has been formed from it and the object it touches or holds, something which was not there before, which is nameless and belongs to no one; and it is this thing with clearly defined limits which now becomes the subject of our attention. This fact is the fundamental explanation of Rodin's manner of grouping figures; it is the source of that extraordinary dependence of the figures on one another, the utter impossibility of dissociating the forms, their refusal to be considered apart. His point of departure is not the figures which embrace one another, he has no models, which he arranges and groups. He begins with surfaces where contact is strongest, as if at points of climax; he starts where something new appears and employs all his understanding of his material in the service of the mysterious phenomena which accompany the birth of what is new. He works as if by the light of flashes occurring at such points and sees only such parts of the entire bodies as are thus illuminated. In the large group of the girl and the man, called

The Kiss, the magic lies in the wise and just distribution of life; we feel as if waves were passing from all these surface-contacts into their bodies, the thrill of beauty, of intuition, and of power. And so it comes about that in every part of these bodies we seem to gaze upon the ecstasy of this kiss; it is like a rising sun, whose light rests everywhere. But still more marvellous is that other kiss about which is raised the statute called *The Eternal Idol*, like walls about a garden. One of the copies of this marble was in the possession of Eugène Carrière, and in the quiet twilight of his home this luminous stone lived like some well-spring, ever filled with the same movement, the rise and fall of magic power. A girl is kneeling. Her lovely body leans gently backward. Her right arm is stretched behind her, and her groping hand has found and holds her foot. Within these three lines, from which no path leads outward, is enclosed her life with its mystery. The stone beneath her raises her kneeling figure. One seems suddenly to recognize in the attitude into which the girl has fallen, in her indolence, reverie or isolation, an ancient sacred posture assumed by some goddess of far-off cruel religions of the past. Her woman's head is inclined forward slightly; with an expression of forbearance, majesty, and patience she gazes down, as if from the height of some silent night, upon the man whose face is buried in her breast as if in many flowers. He too is kneeling, but lower down, low in the stone. His hands are placed behind him, like worthless, empty things. The right lies open, showing its inner side. From this group there goes forth a mysterious greatness. As so often with Rodin, one does not dare to interpret its meaning. It had thousands. Thoughts pass like shadows over it, and behind each of them it rises new and enigmatic in its lucid and anonymous beauty.

There is something of the atmosphere of a Purgatorio in this work. A heaven is at hand but it is not yet attained; a hell is near which is not yet forgotten. Here again all the radiance emanates from contact, the contact of the two bodies and the contact of the woman with herself.

And the tremendous *Gate of Hell*, at which Rodin has worked for twenty solitary years and which has still to be cast, is but a fresh rendering of this theme of the contact of living and pulsating surfaces. Advancing simultaneously in the discovery of the movement of planes and of their association, Rodin ended by looking for bodies touching at many points, whose contacts were more vehement, more powerful, more unrestrained. The greater the number of possible points of contact between two bodies, the more impatient they were to come together, like two closely related chemicals, the firmer and more organically knit was the new unit which they formed. Scenes from Dante rose up before him. Ugolino and the Wandering Ones. Dante and Vergil jostling one another, the throng of the voluptuous, above whom there rose, like a blasted tree, the greedy gesture of avarice. Centaurs, giants and monsters, sirens, fauns and their consorts, all the wild and savage god-beasts of the pre-Christian forest rose before him. And he began to create. He gave reality to all the figures and forms of Dante's dream, lifted them as it were from the stirred depths of his own memory and gave to each in turn the silent deliverance of material existence. Hundreds of figures and groups were thus created. But the movements, which he found in the words of the poet, belonged to another age; they awoke in the creative artist, who restored them to life, the knowledge of thousands of other movements, gestures of appropriation, of loss, of suffering and of resignation which had been evolved in the intervening years, and his tireless hands went on and on beyond the world of the Florentine poet to ever new gestures and figures.

Thus it came about that none of the drama of Life remained unexplored by this earnest, concentrated worker, who had never sought subjects nor desired anything which lay beyond the range of his own ever-maturing technique: all the depths of nights of Love were revealed to him, all the dark, passionate and sorrowful spaciousness in which, as in a world still heroic, clothing was unknown, in which faces were blotted out and the human body came into its own. With senses at white heat, as a seeker after Life, he entered the great confusion of this struggle, and what he beheld was: Life. No narrow, small, oppressive world encompassed him, but one of space. The atmosphere of the alcoves was completely absent. Here was life, a thousand-fold in every moment, in longing and sorrow, in madness and fear, in loss and gain. Here was desire immeasurable, thirst so great that all the waters of the world dried in it like a single drop, here was neither deception nor denial, and here the gestures of giving and of receiving were real, were great. Here were vices and blasphemies, damnation and bliss, and suddenly one understood that a world which concealed and hid all this, which treated it as if it did not exist, must indeed be poor. It did exist. Running parallel with the whole history of the human race, there was this other history, innocent of covering, of convention, of rank and class—which knew only conflict. It, too, had had its historical development. From being a mere instinct, it had become a longing, from being an appetite between man and woman, it had become a desire of one human being for another. And as such it appears in Rodin's work. It is still the eternal conflict of the sexes, but woman is no longer the forced or willing animal. Like man, she is awake and filled with longing, it is as though the two made common cause to find their souls. He who rises in the night and quietly seeks another is like a digger for treasure seeking the great happiness, which is so indispensable, at the crossroads of sex. There is something of the longing which makes great poets in all vice, in all lustful sins against nature, in all the desperate and vain attempts to find an eternal meaning for life. Here is humanity's hunger reaching out beyond itself; stretching out hands towards eternity. Here eyes open which gaze upon death without fear; here a hopeless heroism is revealed, whose glory is transient as a smile, blossoming and perishing like a rose. Here are the storms of desire, the calm of expectation; here are dreams which become deeds, and deeds which pass away in dreams. Here, as at some gigantic gambling-table, a man's whole endowment of strength is lost and won. All this is found in Rodin's work. He, who knew so much of life already, found here all life's fullness and abundance. He found bodies expressing will in every part, and mouths whose very form was a cry, rising as it seemed from the deep places of the earth. He found the gestures of the primitive gods, the beauty and litheness of animals, the intoxication of ancient dances, and the movements of forgotten religious rites strangely joined to the new gestures which had developed in the long period during which art had been inattentive and blind to all these revelations. These new gestures had a peculiar interest for him. They were impatient. Like one who searches in vain for some desired object and, not knowing where to turn, becomes more and more distracted and hasty, disturbing all about him and gathering round him a disorderly mass of things as if to compel them to join in the search, so the gestures of humanity, failing to understand their own significance, have become more impatient, more nervous, more hurried, and more abrupt. And all the tormented questions of existence lie about them. But at the same time these movements have become more hesitating. They no longer possess the athletic and resolute directness which characterized the appropriating gestures of earlier generations. They are not like the movements preserved for us in ancient statues, of which only the beginning and the end were important. Between these two simple points innumerable moments of transition have arisen, and it was clear that the life of the modern man, when he was active as well as when he felt himself incapable of action, was spent in these transitionary states. The gestures of seizing, of beckoning, of relinquishing, and of holding had changed. All of them showed greater experience and, at the same time, greater ignorance; much less courage and a constant attacking of obstacles; much more mourning for what has been lost; much more calculation, judgment, reflexion, and less spontaneity. Rodin formed such gestures. He made them from one or more figures, forming them into things after his own manner. He imparted to hundreds and hundreds of figures scarcely larger than his own hand the life which is in all passion, the florescence of all desire and the burden of all vice. He created bodies touching at all points and clinging together like animals at deadly grips with one another, falling into the depth as one single object; bodies which were like listening human faces and like arms about to strike; chains of bodies, garlands and tendrils, and figures like heavy bunches of grapes, into which the sweetness of sin rose from the roots of pain. The only other artist who has treated bodily contacts with the same surpassing power is Leonardo, in his grandiose version of the end of the world. Here as there we have figures flinging themselves into the abyss in order to escape from the thought of the great woe and others who dash out their children's brains that they may not live to know it.

The army of these figures had grown much too numerous to fit into the frame and wings of the *Gate of Hell*. Rodin made repeated selections. He excluded everything which was too solitary to adapt itself to the great whole, everything not absolutely essential in that connexion. He let the figures and groups find their own places; he observed the life of the multitude which he had created, watched each individually and acted in accordance with the will of each. Thus did the world of this Gate grow gradually. Its surfaces, to which the plastic forms were attached, began to live; in reliefs of decreasing depth the agitation of the figures melted into the surface. The chief movement within the frame is a rising up from both sides, an upward strive and lift, in the wings of the Gate a falling, a downward glide and rush. The wings recede slightly and their upper edge is separated from the protruding edge of the cross-frame by a fairly large surface. In front of this, set within the quiet, enclosed space, is the figure of the *Thinker*, the man who sees the whole immensity and all the terrors of this spectacle because he thinks it. He sits silent and lost in meditation, heavy with visions and thoughts, and, with his whole strength (the strength of a man of action), he thinks. His whole body has become a skull and all the blood in his veins has become brain. He forms the centre of the Gate, although there are three other male figures standing above him on the top of the frame. The depth has the effect of making them appear in distance. Their heads are bent together, the three arms outstretched meet in the middle pointing downward towards the same spot below them, towards the abyss, which draws them downwards as by its weight. But the *Thinker* has to bear this weight within himself.

Amongst the groups and figures to which this Gate gave rise, there are many of great beauty. It is as little possible to enumerate them all as it is to describe them. Rodin himself once said he would have to talk for a year if he were to attempt to reproduce one of his works in words. We can only say that, like many of the small figures of animals of the antique, these little images, in plaster, bronze and stone, give the impression of being quite large. In Rodin's studio there is a cast of a panther, of Greek workmanship, scarcely the size of a hand (the original is in the medallion case of the *Bibliothèque Nationale* in Paris); if you look from the front under its body into the space formed by the four strong lithe limbs, you can imagine you are looking into the depth of an Indian rock temple; so does this work grow and expand to the size of the proportions it suggests. The same is true of Rodin's small plastic figures. By giving them many surfaces, innumerable, perfect and definite planes, he creates an effect of magnitude. The air plays round them as about a rock. When they have an upward movement they seem to be lifting the very heavens, and with the downward movement of their fall they seem to bring the stars down with them.

Possibly the *Danaïde*, flinging herself from a kneeling position into her flowing hair, belongs to the same period. It is wonderful to pass slowly round this marble, to follow the long, long way which passes from the full, rich curve of the back to the face losing itself in the stone as in a great weeping, to the hand resting deep in the eternal ice of the marble yet speaking softly, like a last dying flower, of life. And *Illusion, the Daughter of Ikarus*, that dazzling embodiment of a long, helpless fall. And the lovely group called *Man and his Thought*. The representation of a man in kneeling posture awakening, by the touch of his brow on the stone before him, the softly indicated form of a woman still imprisoned in the stone; if we may venture on interpretation, we must rejoice over the idea here expressed, that thought is inseparable from the brow of man: for what stands living before him is only his own thought; immediately behind is stone. Closely related to this work is the head, rising meditative and calm from a great block on which the chin rests, *Thought*, this clarity, this existence, this face rising slowly out of the heavy sleep of inanimate continuity. And then the *Caryatide*. Here we have no longer an upright figure bearing with ease or difficulty the burden of a stone, beneath which it simply took up its position after the stone was fixed; it is the nude figure of a woman, kneeling, bent, crouching low, her position caused by the burden whose weight appears in all her limbs like the continued act of falling. On every smallest part of this body the whole stone rests like some will greater, more ancient, more powerful than the body, whose destiny to support the weight does not, however, cease. It bears it as in a dream one bears the impossible, finding no escape. And in this crushed and helpless attitude there is still the act of supporting a weight, and when weariness again overtakes it, forcing it into a lying posture, even then the recumbent attitude will still express the bearing of a burden without end. Such is the *Caryatide*.

It is possible, if one so desires, to explain and illuminate most of Rodin's works by associating ideas with them. For those who are unaccustomed to approaching beauty by the way of simple contemplation and find it too difficult, there are other, less direct ways, through interpretations, which are noble, great, and full of significance. It is as if the infinite rightness and trueness of these figures, the perfect equilibrium of all their movements, the marvellous inner justice of their proportions, the way in which they are imbued with life, as if all this, which makes them into things of beauty, endowed them also with the power to be unsurpassable embodiments of the themes which the master called up when he named them. With Rodin subject matter is never attached to a work of art like an animal to a tree. It has its existence somewhere in the neighbourhood of the work and lives by it, somewhat like the custodian of a museum. Much may be learnt from such a person on application; but if one can get on without him one is freer, less disturbed, and in the end better informed.

When the first inspiration comes from the subject matter, when the impulse to create is given by a classic legend, part of a poem, a scene from history or some actual person, such material is transformed more and more, once Rodin begins to work upon it, into something concrete and anonymous: translated into the language of the hands, the demands which then arise all have a new meaning, which depends solely on the conditions of plastic realization.

This process of forgetting and transforming the original subject takes place by anticipation in Rodin's drawings. He has developed his own medium of expression in this art also, so that these sketches (there are many hundreds of them) give an independent and original revelation of his personality.

Dating from his early period, there are the wash-drawings, with amazingly strong light and shade effects, such as the famous *Man with the Bull,* suggestive of Rembrandt, or the head of the young St. John the Baptist, or the shrieking mask of the Genius of War; all jottings and studies which helped the artist to understand the life of planes and their relationship to the atmosphere. Then there are figures drawn with dashing confidence, forms filled out by all their contours, drawn with many quick strokes of the pen, and others enclosed within the melody of a single vibrating outline which depicts a movement with unforgettable purity of expression. Of such a kind are the drawings with which Rodin illustrated a copy of the *Fleurs du mal* at the request of a collector of taste. We say nothing when we speak of a most profound understanding of Baudelairean verse; we say more when we recall how these poems, in their complete self-saturation, allow of no addition, no heightening of effect: that one is aware of both amplification and enhancement when Rodin's lines interpret them is an indication of the irresistible beauty of the drawings. The pen-sketch illustrating the poem *La mort des pauvres* reaches out beyond these sublime verses with such a simple and ever growing greatness that it seems to fill the whole world from the rising to the going down of the sun.

It is the same with the drypoint etchings, in which the movement of infinitely delicate lines surrounds with its fluidity the essence of a reality, like the extreme outline of some beautiful glass object which is itself, at any given moment, clearly defined.

Finally, there are those strange documents of what is momentary, of what is almost imperceptible as it passes. Rodin had the theory that if insignificant movements of the model, when he believed himself to be unobserved, were caught rapidly, they would give a vividness of expression of which we have no idea because we are not accustomed to follow them with keen, alert attention. Keeping his eye constantly on the model and leaving the paper entirely to his experienced and rapid hand, he drew an immense number of movements which till then had been neither seen nor recorded, and it turned out that they had a vitality of expression which was tremendous; associations of movement appeared which had hitherto been overlooked and unrecognized, and they possessed all the directness, force, and warmth of pure animal life. A brush of ochre passed with varying pressure rapidly over the outline produced in the enclosed surface such an incredibly strong effect of modelling that one seemed to have before one plastic figures of baked clay. And once again a whole new vista filled with nameless life had been discovered; deep places, over which all others had passed with echoing steps, yielded their waters to him in whose hands the willow-rod had prophesied.

So, too, with portraits,—the rendering of the subject first in drawing formed part of the preparations by which Rodin proceeded slowly and with inner concentration to the final work. For, mistaken as it is to see in his plastic art a form of Impressionism, it was none the less the mass of exact and boldly seized impressions which provided him with the wealth of material from which he finally selected what was important and essential, to unite it in one perfect synthetic whole. When he passes from the bodies, which he explores and forms, to the faces, he must often feel as if he were stepping from some wide and windy space into a room filled with people: here everything is crowded and dark, and there is the feeling of an interior beneath the arching brows and in the shadow about the mouth. Whereas one sees in the bodies constant change and the rhythm of waves, ebb and flow, in the faces there is atmosphere. As in a room where much has happened, where there has been joy and fear, sorrow and hope. And no experience has quite passed away, none has been superseded by the other; each has taken its place beside the other, has remained to wither like a flower in water. But he who comes from without, from the great wind, brings space into the chamber with him.

The mask of the *Man with the Broken Nose* was Rodin's first likeness. His manner of experiencing a face is fully developed in this work, we feel how unconditionally he devoted himself to the subject before him, we see his reverence for every line drawn in by destiny, his confidence in Life which creates even where it mars. He made the *Man with the Broken Nose* in a sort of blind faith, without asking who the man was, whose life was lived through afresh in his hands. He made him as God made the first man, without other purpose than to create life itself, anonymous life. With ever growing knowledge, experience, and power he returned to the creation of human faces. He could not behold their features without thinking of the days which had been at work upon them, of that great army of labourers ceaselessly busied about a face as though it could never be finished. Thus from quietly and conscientiously reproducing life, the artist in his maturity learned, at first hesitatingly and experimentally and then with ever bolder confidence, to interpret the writing with which the faces were completely covered. He gave no play to his imagination; he invented nothing. Not for a moment did he scorn the slowness of his medium. It would have been so easy to take wings of some sort and outstrip it. As always, he kept step beside it, walking the great distances which had to be covered, walking like the ploughman behind his plough. But whilst he ploughed his furrows, he meditated on the land and on its hidden places, on the sky above it, on the passage of the winds, and on the fall of the rains, on everything that was and wrought harm and passed and returned and did not cease to be. And, less distracted by the multiplicity of things, he felt himself better able to recognize in all this the eternal, that which made suffering a good, travail a bringing forth of life, and pain beautiful.

This interpretation, which began with the portraits, took ever deeper root in his work. It forms the last stage, the extreme limit of his great development. Its beginning was slow. Rodin entered upon this new way with infinite caution. Once again he advanced from plane to plane, following Nature and listening to her voice. It was she herself who showed him, as it were, the places about which he knew more than could be seen. By beginning with these and producing from many confused details a great simplification, he did what Christ did for the people when, with a sublime parable, He cleansed of their guilt those who came questioning Him blindly. He carried out one of Nature's purposes. He completed something which was helpless to develop of itself, he revealed hidden relationships, as the evening of a misty day reveals the mountains rolling their great undulations into the far distance.

Full of the living burden of his great knowledge, he looked into the faces of those about him like one who knows the future. This gives to his portraits their extraordinarily clear definiteness, but also that prophetic greatness which, in the statues of Victor Hugo and of Balzac, rises to an indescribable perfection. To create a likeness meant for him to seek eternity in some given face, that part of eternity by which the face participated in the great life of eternal things. He made none which he did not lift a little from its place into the future; as we hold an object against the sky in order to see its form with greater clarity and simplicity. This is not what we call beautifying a thing, nor is it right to speak of giving it characteristic expression. It is more than that; it is the separating of the permanent from the ephemeral, the passing of a judgment, the executing of justice.

His likenesses, even apart from the etchings, include a very great number of works which are masterly in their perfection. There are busts in plaster, bronze, marble, and sandstone, heads in baked clay and masks which have simply been allowed to dry. Portraits of women occur repeatedly in all his periods. The famous bust in the Luxembourg Museum is one of the earliest. It is filled with a peculiar and beautiful life and has a certain feminine charm, but many later works excel it in simplicity and in concentration of the planes. It is, perhaps, the only one of Rodin's works which does not owe its entire beauty to excellences peculiar to the sculptor, for part of its life comes from that spirit of grace which has been inherent in the plastic art of France for centuries. It is distinguished by the elegance which characterizes even bad sculpture of the French tradition; it is not entirely free from that gallantry in representing the *belle femme* which the serious and penetrative genius of Rodin soon left far behind. But it is well to remind oneself at this point that he had to overcome this inherited attitude of mind, that he had to suppress an innate facility in order to start completely poor. But he did not need, on that account, to cease to be French: the great masters of the cathedrals were French.

The later portraits of women have a different, a more profound, a less commonplace beauty. We should, perhaps, mention that it was mostly foreigners, Americans, whom Rodin portrayed. There is marvellous work in some of these portraits, pure as antique cameos which it would seem sacrilege to touch. There are faces whose smile is nowhere defined but which plays over the features with so veil-like a softness that it seems to rise with every taking of the breath. Enigmatically closed lips and wide, dreaming eyes which gaze past everything into an eternal moonlit night. And withal, Rodin appears by preference to regard a woman's face as part of her beautiful body, as though he would make the eyes the eyes of her body and the mouth the mouthpiece of her body. When he thus creates and sees a whole, the face becomes endowed with so strong and moving an expression of unsuspected life that he far surpasses his heads of women, although the latter may appear to be much more carefully executed.

In the male portraits his procedure is different. A man's being can be more easily thought of as concentrated within the limits of his face. One can even imagine moments (such as moments of repose or of inner excitement) when all his life comes into his face. Rodin chooses such moments, when he gives us the likeness of a man; or rather, he creates them. He goes far afield. He attaches little importance to the first impression, or to the second, and none at all to those that follow. He observes and notes. He notes movements which are too insignificant to be put into words, turns and half-turns, forty foreshortenings and eighty profiles. He catches his model unawares, in habitual or accidental attitudes, under the stress of effort and whilst a prey to lassitude, seizing every incipient expression. He knows every transitory expression of feature, knows whence comes the smile and whither it departs. He lives through a human face as through the scene of some drama in which he himself takes part; his place is in the midst of it, and nothing that occurs is indifferent to him or escapes him. He refuses to be told anything about the person, he wants to know only what he sees. But he sees everything.

And so much time is spent on each bust. The material grows, partly in the form of sketches caught with a few strokes of the pen and a few touches of colour wash, partly stored up in the memory; for Rodin has made of his memory both a reliable and a ready agent. His eye sees a great deal more during the sittings than he can carry out at the time. He forgets none of it, and often his real work begins after the departure of the model, when he works from a well-stored memory. His memory is wide and capacious; his impressions do not undergo any change there, but they accustom themselves to their surroundings, and when they pass thence into his hands they seem to be but the natural gestures of those hands.

This mode of work leads to tremendous creations composed of hundreds upon hundreds of vital moments: and such is, indeed, the impression we receive from these busts. The many widely separated contrasts and the unexpected transitions, which go to make up a human being and his continuous development, meet here in felicitous union and are knit together by an inner force of adhesion. These people have been created from material brought from the most distant reaches of their personality, all the climates of their temperament are revealed in the hemispheres of their head. There is the sculptor Dalou, whose face vibrates with tenacious and jealous energy and with nervous fatigue, there is Henri Rochefort's romantic mask, Octave Mirabeau, revealing behind the man of action the dreams and longings of the poet, and Puvis de Chavannes and Victor Hugo, whom Rodin knew so well, and above all there is the indescribably lovely bronze, the bust of the painter Jean-Paul Laurens. This bust is, perhaps, the finest thing in the Luxembourg Museum.[1] It shows such profound and at the same time such grandly conceived treatment of surface, it is so restrained in pose, so powerful in expression, so alert and full of movement that one cannot escape the feeling that Nature herself has taken this work out of the hands of the sculptor to preserve it as one of her most precious possessions. The magnificent patina, through the dark smoke-coloured surface of which the metal shines like shooting flames of fire, contributes not a little to the perfection of this work's uncanny beauty.

There is also a bust of Bastien-Lepage, beautiful and melancholy, showing the suffering artist who in all he did expressed one long farewell to his work. It was executed for Damvillers, the little village of his birth, and has been placed in the churchyard there. So it is really a memorial. And all Rodin's busts have something monumental about them in their completeness and breadth of conception. Only in this one there is greater simplification of planes and a still more careful selection of essentials with a view to the effect from a distance. The monuments which Rodin created tended more and more to fulfil these requirements. He began with the memorial to Claude Gelée for Nancy; and from this first interesting attempt there is a steep ascent to the grandiose achievement of the *Balzac*.

Many of Rodin's memorial works have gone to America, the finest being destroyed in the Chilean disturbances before ever it was placed in position. This was the equestrian statue of General Lynch. Like the lost masterpiece of Leonardo which it resembled, perhaps, in its power of expression and the

[1] Now in the Rodin Museum (*Translator's Note*).

marvellously vital oneness of horse and rider, this statue was destined not to survive. To judge from a little plaster cast in the Rodin Museum at Meudon, it must have consisted of the plastic figure of a lean man erect in the saddle, with an air of command which he wears, not with the brutal arrogance of a condottiere, but with nervous tension, more like one who exercises his authority as a duty lying outside his own personal life. Here we see the forward-pointing hand of the general rising out of the entire mass of the statue composed of man and beast; the same feature gives to the gesture of Victor Hugo its unforgettable majesty, its sweeping significance, this force which compels belief at first sight. The great living hand of an aged man holding converse with the ocean does not go forth from the poet alone; it comes from the summit of the whole group, as if from a mountain on which it had been praying ere it spoke. Victor Hugo is here the exile, the solitary of Guernsey, and it is one of the miracles of the statue that the Muses surrounding him do not appear as figures visiting the lonely man: they are rather his solitude itself made visible. Rodin has achieved this effect by revealing the hidden life of the individual figures and, so to say, by concentrating upon the poet's inner experiences; here, by once again giving individual life to the points of contact, he has succeeded in making these marvellously living figures seem a medium of expression for the man who is seated. They are about him like great gestures he has once made, gestures so young and beautiful that they have been endowed by some goddess with immortality and will endure forever in the form of beautiful women.

For the figure of the poet himself Rodin made many studies. Hidden in a window niche of the Hôtel Lusignan during Victor Hugo's receptions, he observed and noted down hundreds upon hundreds of the aged poet's movements and every expression of his animated countenance. As a result of these preparations we have the various portraits of Victor Hugo by Rodin. For the statue he needed to immerse himself still more deeply in his subject. He put from him the host of individual impressions and looked at them from a distance, as a whole; and as one figure, that of Homer, was possibly created from a succession of rhapsodes, so he created this one likeness from all the pictures present in his memory. And to this one, final likeness he imparted the impressive greatness of legend; as if all this might indeed have been only a myth, and its source some great rock towering up fantastically out of the sea, in the strange outlines of which forgotten peoples had seen a sleeping gesture.

Rodin has always shown this power of lifting the past into the realm of the permanent when historical characters or facts seek to live again through his art; most triumphantly, perhaps, in the *Burghers of Calais*. In this case, historical fact was limited to a few columns in the Chronicle of Froissart. It was the story of how the town of Calais was besieged by the English king, Edward III; how the king refused to pardon the town which was overcome by the fear of hunger; how he finally agreed to raise the siege if six of the chief burghers would deliver themselves into his hands, "that he may do with them according to his will". And he required that they should leave the town bare-headed, clad only in their shirts, with a rope round their necks and the keys of the town and fortress in their hand. The chronicler then describes the scene within the town; he reports how the burgomaster, messire Jean de Vienne, causes the bells to be rung and how the burghers assemble in the market place. They have heard the dread message and wait in silence. But already the heroes, the chosen ones, stand out from amongst them, feeling within themselves the call to death. At this point the wailing and weeping of the crowd can be heard in the words of the chronicler. He himself seems for a moment to be moved and to write with trembling pen. But he controls himself. He mentions two of the heroes by name, two he forgets. Of one he says that he was the richest burgher in the town, of the second, that he had position and wealth and "two beautiful damsels for daughters", of the third he knows only that he was rich in possessions and inheritance, and of the fourth that he was the brother of the third. He tells us that they laid aside all but their shirts, that they fastened ropes round their necks and that they set out thus with the keys of the town and the fortress.

He tells how they came into the camp of the king; he describes how harshly the king received them, how the executioner was standing waiting beside them when, at the request of the queen, the monarch granted them their lives. "He attended to the words of his wife," says Froissart, "because she was with child." More the chronicle does not relate.

But this material sufficed for Rodin. He felt immediately that there was a point in this story at which something great happened, something apart from time and names, something independent of circumstance, something simple. He turned all his attention upon the moment of their setting forth. He saw these men as they started on their way; he felt how the whole life that each had lived was at that moment present within him, how each stood laden with the life of his past, ready to bear it forth out of the ancient city. Six men rose up before him, of whom no two were alike; only two were brothers, between whom there was possibly a certain likeness. But each had come to his decision in his own way and lived through this last hour in his own manner, with solemn rejoicing of spirit and suffering of the body, which clung to life. And then he ceased to behold these figures. In his memory there rose up gestures, gestures of renunciation, of farewell, of relinquishment. Endless gestures. He collected them. He formed them all. They flowed towards him out of the fullness of his knowledge. It was as if a hundred heroic figures rose up within his memory, eager for the sacrifice. And he accepted the whole hundred and made of them six. He formed them nude, each by itself, in all the communicativeness of their shivering bodies. More than life size, in the natural proportion of their resolve.

He created the aged man with hanging, loose-jointed arms; and he gave him the heavy, trailing step, the worn-out walk of an old man and an expression of weariness which flows over his face into his beard.

He created the man carrying the key. There is life in him for many years to come and it is all concentrated in this last sudden hour. He can scarcely support it. His lips are pressed together, his hands bite into the key. He has set his strength on fire and it is burning within him, in his defiance. He created the man who holds his bowed head in both hands as if to collect himself, to be alone for one more moment. He created the two brothers, one of whom looks backward, whilst the other bows his head with a movement of decision and submission, as if already offering it to the executioner.

And he created the vague gesture of the man "passing through life". Gustave Geffroy called him the "Passer-by". As he advances he turns back, not to the town, not to the weeping people, nor to those accompanying him. He turns back to himself. His right arm is raised in an uncertain curve; his hand opens in the air and lets something go, somewhat in the way in which we set free a bird. He is taking leave of all uncertainty, of all happiness still unrealized, of the suffering which will now wait in vain, of men living somewhere whom he might have met, of all that days to come might have brought with them, and he takes leave also of that death which he had thought to be far away, gentle and silent, which he thought to meet after many, many days. This figure, if placed by itself in some old shady garden, would make a monument for all who have died young.

And so Rodin has given to each of these men life in the final gesture of his life. The single figures are sublime in their simple greatness. They recall Donatello and perhaps still more Claux Sluter and his prophets in the Chartreuse of Dijon.

One's first impression is that Rodin has done nothing further to unite them. He has given them the same costume, the shirt and the rope, and has placed them beside each other in two rows; the three who are going forward, in the first row, the others, turning towards the right, behind, as if in the act of joining them. The position for which the statue was intended, was the market place of Calais, the same spot from which the sad pilgrimage once began. There these silent figures were to stand, raised only a little above the daily life of the town by a low platform, as if the dread procession might still, at any time, begin.

But, because it was contrary to custom, a low socle was

considered unsuitable at Calais. And Rodin proposed a different placing of it. He suggested a square tower built close by the sea, as broad as the base of the statue, with plain hewn walls two stories high, and upon this the six burghers were to be placed in the solitude of wind and sky. As might have been foreseen, this proposal had no better chance of acceptance. And yet it was in accordance with the very spirit of the work. Had it been tried, it would have afforded an incomparable opportunity of admiring the unity of the group, which, although composed of six figures, yet appeared as one single object, so closely interdependent were its parts. And withal the single figures did not touch one another, they stood side by side, like the last remaining trees of a forest which has been felled, and the only thing uniting them was the air, which bore a quite peculiar relationship to them. Passing round the group, one was amazed to see how the gestures rose pure and great from out the rhythm of the contours, how they rose, stood still and fell back into the mass, like flags being furled. Everything was clear and definite. There appeared to be no room for accident of any kind. Like all Rodin's groups, this one was self-contained, a world within itself, a whole, filled with life which circulated within it and nowhere passed outside or lost itself. In place of contacts we have here the overlapping of contours, which is, indeed, a kind of contact, immensely reduced through the medium of the intervening air which acts upon and modifies them. There are contacts with distance between, meeting-points, the passing of one form in front of another, such as are seen at times in masses of clouds or amongst mountains, where the air is not a dividing abyss but rather a gradual transition, suggestive of direction.

The participation of the atmosphere had always been an important factor for Rodin. He had made all his things, plane for plane, in relationship to space, and this gave them that greatness and independence, that indescribable maturity, which distinguished them from all other works. But now, having gradually learnt, in his interpretation of nature, to emphasize expression, it appeared that, in doing so, he had also intensified the relationship of the atmosphere to his statue, so that it surrounded the interdependent planes more vividly, as it were, more passionately. Whereas formerly his works stood in the midst of space, it now seemed as if space snatched them to itself. Only in some of the animals on the cathedrals can a like effect be seen. With respect to them also the atmosphere plays a special part; it appears calm or filled with wind according as it passes over places showing emphasis or the reverse. And, indeed, when Rodin gave unity to his works by the climaxes of the planes, when he increased elevations and gave greater depths to hollows, he dealt with his sculpture as the atmosphere had dealt with the things exposed to it throughout the centuries. It too had imparted unity, had deepened and covered with dust, by rain and frost, by sun and storm had fitted these things for a life less swiftly lived, a darkling, soaring, enduring life.

Rodin had arrived in his own manner at this effect in the *Burghers of Calais*; it contains the monumental principle of his art. By such means he was able to create things which were visible afar off, things surrounded not merely by the immediate atmosphere but by heaven itself. With one living surface he could catch and reflect the distances as with a mirror and could form a gesture which appeared immense, forcing space to participate in it.

Such is the slim youth kneeling with arms flung upward and backward in a gesture of infinite appeal. Rodin called this figure *The Prodigal Son*, but, without our knowing how it happens, it suddenly assumes the name of *Prayer*. And that, too, it soon outgrows. This is no figure of a son kneeling to his father. This attitude makes a God necessary, and in the figure thus kneeling are present all who need Him. All space belongs to this marble; it is alone in the world.

The same is true of *Balzac*. Rodin has given him proportions which are probably much greater than those of the writer's figure. He has understood the very essence of his nature, but he has not stopped with the limits of that nature; he has drawn this mighty contour about its ultimate, its most distant possibilities, about its unfulfilment, a contour which would seem to have been prefigured in the gravestones of long perished races.

For years he lived engrossed by this figure. He visited Balzac's home, the landscape of Touraine, which constantly re-appears in his books, he read his letters, studied the existing portraits of Balzac, and he lived through his works again and again; on all the many branching and winding ways of his work he encountered Balzac's people, whole families and generations, a world which seemed to have an unmoved faith in the existence of its creator, to live with his life and with its gaze to look upon him. He saw that all these thousand people, let them do what they would, were entirely occupied with the one person, their creator. And as one can, perchance, guess from the various facial expressions of the spectators what a drama is about, which is taking place upon the stage, so he searched in all these faces for the personality which for them was still alive. He believed, like Balzac, in the reality of this world and succeeded in taking his place in it for a while. He lived in it as if he were himself one of Balzac's creations, unobtrusively inserted amongst the multitude of existences which Balzac had created. In this way he learnt most. Other available material appeared very much less eloquent. The daguerreotypes afforded only evidence of a quite general kind and nothing new. The face they showed was familiar from one's school-days. Only one of the portraits, originally in the possession of Stephan Mallarmé, which shows Balzac coatless and with braces, was more characteristic. And then the records of his contemporaries were pressed into service. Théophile Gautier's words, jottings of the Goncourts, and Lamartine's fine pen-picture of Balzac. Besides these there was only the bust by David in the Comédie Française and a small likeness by Louis Boulanger.

Filled with the spirit of Balzac, Rodin now proceeded, by means of this material, to build up the outward appearance. He used living models of similar bodily proportions and made seven figures in different attitudes, which he carried out completely. He employed stout, square-set men with heavy limbs and short arms, and after these preliminary studies he made a Balzac conceived very much as he is depicted in the Nadar daguerreotype. He felt, however, that he had not yet achieved anything final. He reverted to Lamartine's description. There he read: "He had the countenance of an element" and "He had so much spiritual vitality that it carried the heavy body with complete ease". Rodin felt that a great part of the problem lay in those words. He got nearer to its solution by seeking to clothe all the seven figures in monkish garb such as Balzac was in the habit of wearing at his work. The result was a Balzac dressed in a cowl, much too private, too withdrawn into the silence of his disguise.

But Rodin's vision grew slowly as it passed from one form to another. And at last he saw him. It was a broad, striding figure, whose heaviness was completely lost in the fall of the cloak. The hair was supported by the strong neck and the face lay back upon the hair, gazing, and, in the intoxication of its gaze, seething with creative power; the face of an element. That was Balzac in the fertility of his abundance, the founder of generations, the squanderer of destinies. That was the man whose eye needed no objects; whose glance would have furnished the world had it been empty. That was the man who thought to become rich through legendary silver-mines and happy in a foreign love. That was Creation itself, assuming the figure of Balzac that it might appear in visible form; the presumption, the arrogance, the ecstasy, the intoxication of creation. The head, thrown back, crowned this figure like those spheres which dance upon the jets of fountains. All heaviness had become light and rose and fell.

It was thus that Rodin had seen his Balzac in a moment of tremendous concentration and tragic exaggeration, and thus he depicted him. The vision did not pass; it was transformed.

This development of Rodin's, which surrounded the large, monumental pieces of his work with space, endowed the others also with a new beauty. It gave them a peculiar nearness. Amongst the more recent works there are small groups which owe their effect to the unity in their composition and to the wonderfully tender treatment of the marble. These marbles retain, even in full daylight, the mysterious shimmer which emanates from white objects in twilight. This is due not solely to the vitality of the points of contact; flat marble bands have been left here and there between the figures and between their individual parts, like cross-pieces, uniting one form with another in the background. Nor is this accidental. These blocks prevent useless vistas which would carry the eye beyond the object into empty space; their effect is to preserve the rounded contours of the forms which would otherwise appear sharp and clean-cut against such gaps. They collect the light as in a bowl from which there is a constant gentle overflow. If Rodin aimed at drawing the air as close as possible to the surface of his work, it is as though the object in these cases actually melted into the air: the marble seems to be only the firm, fruitful kernel and its ultimate, most delicate contour to be the vibrating air. The light which comes to this marble has no will of its own; it does not pass on to other objects; it clings to the marble, lingers, delays, dwells within it.

This blocking of unessential vistas was a kind of approach to relief. And Rodin is, in fact, planning an immense bas-relief which shall unite in itself all the light effects already achieved in the smaller groups. His idea is to make a lofty column with a broad band of relief winding upwards round it. Running alongside these spirals there will rise an interior winding staircase with arcades on the outward side. Within, the figures on the walls will live as it were in their own atmosphere, and the result will be a piece of plastic showing the secret of *clair-obscur*, a statue of the twilight, akin to the sculptures which stand in the vestibules of ancient cathedrals.

This is how he plans his *Tower of Labour*. On the slowly rising relief will be shown the history of labour. The long scroll will begin in a crypt, showing those who grow old in mines, and as it moves upwards it will pass through all the forms of human occupation, from the noisy and vigorous to the more and more silent, from blast furnaces to the human heart, from hammers to the human brain. There will be two tall figures at the entrance, Day and Night, and on the summit two winged genii, figures of blessing descending from bright spheres to rest upon the tower. For this monument to labour is to take the form of a tower. Rodin does not think of representing labour by any great figure or gesture; it is not visible from afar. Its place is in factories, in work-rooms, within the brain; in hidden places. He knows, for it is so with his own work; and he works incessantly. His life passes like a single working-day.

He has several studios; some better known than others, where visitors and correspondence find him, and others out of the way and known to none. Bare, poor cells, filled with dust and greyness. But their poverty is like the great, grey poverty of God, in which the trees in March awaken. There is something of early spring about it; a quiet promise and a deep solemnity.

Some day, perhaps, the Tower of Labour will take form in one of these work-rooms. At present, while it is still unrealized, one can only speak of its significance; and that appeared to be in the concrete material. But once the work is there, we shall feel that, in this as in his other works, Rodin has not aimed at anything beyond his art. The body at work has revealed itself to him, as earlier the body in love. It has been a new revelation of Life. But this creative genius lives so entirely in the midst of his creations, so immersed in his work, that he can never see such revelations in any other form than in the simple medium of his own art. New life means for him neither more nor less than new planes, new gestures. So simple has life become about him. He can no longer go wrong.

By virtue of this development Rodin has acted as a signpost to all the Arts in this confused age.

Some day men will understand what it was that made this great artist so great, the fact, namely, that he was a worker who desired nothing but to participate with all his powers in the humble and difficult existence of his medium. This implied a certain renunciation of life; but just by the patience of such renunciation did he win life: for the world offered itself to his chisel.

PREFATORY REMARK

Some may think it a parsimonious exploitation of something already in existence if the text of a lecture (frequently in the form in which it was delivered, though amplified by more than half) is here being offered in print. As, however, the ideas contained in that context continue to be valid, there is no reason to deprive them of the original form of their expression; it is all the more natural. For it is not just in the application of those ideas but in their essence that there is appeal: they want to be heard. They really want to speak, and to many, and they want to try to mediate between one life or another and a very great art. This intention will come as no surprise; it scarcely differs from the many similar intentions now at work, most of them achieving success or recognition. Interest in things artistic has increased. Studios have become more accessible and more communicative vis-à-vis a criticism that can no longer be accused of being backward; the art trade itself has abandoned its prejudices and, oddly enough, placed itself at the head of a development in which the public can now readily participate: by its criticism and by its willingness to buy. This attitude, however – welcome and progressive though it may be – bypasses an œuvre such as Rodin's; it skips over it, it scarcely touches it.

The realization that this extensive and still inadequately elucidated work is unattainable to mere interest was the motivation for this lecture. It will perhaps justify its publication.

Paris, July 1907

SECOND PART

THERE are some great names which, if they were pronounced at this moment, would establish a friendship between us, a cordiality, a unanimity, which would make it seem as if I—only apparently isolated—were speaking from amongst you, my voice sounding from your midst as one of your voices. But the name which shines like a great five-starred constellation high above us this evening, cannot be spoken. Not now. It would bring unrest amongst you, would set in motion currents of sympathy and of hostility, whereas I need your tranquillity and the unruffled surface of your friendly expectation.

I beg those who are still able to do so to forget the name in question, and I require of all a still wider forgetting. You are accustomed to hear art spoken about, and who would conceal the fact that you give an ever readier reception to words which speak to you on that subject? A certain beautiful and vigorous movement, which could not be hidden any longer, has arrested your gaze like the flight of a great bird: and now you are asked to lower your eyes for the space of an evening. For it is not in that direction, not towards the firmament of uncertain developments, that I would turn your attention, not from the bird flight of the new art that I would prophesy to you. I am as one who would remind you of your childhood. No, not only of your own childhood, but of everything that ever was childhood. For my purpose is to awaken memories in you which are not yours, which are older than you; to restore connexions and renew relationships which lie in the distant past.

If my subject were personalities, I could begin where you have just left off on entering this room; breaking in upon your conversation, I would, without effort, share your thoughts—borne and swept along by this stirring age, on the shores of which all human interests seem to lie, washed by its waters and strangely reflected in them. But when I attempt to visualize my task, it becomes clear to me that it is not people about whom I have to speak, but things.

Things.

When I say that word (do you hear?), there is a silence; the silence which surrounds things. All movement subsides and becomes contour, and out of past and future time something permanent is formed: space, the great calm of objects which know no urge.

But no, you do not yet feel the silence falling. The word "things" passes you by, it has no meaning for you: it means too much, all of which lacks significance. And so I am glad I have appealed to childhood; perhaps it will help me to bring home to you this word, as something precious linked with many memories.

If possible, out of practice and grown-up as your feelings are, bring them back to any one of your childhood's possessions, with which you were familiar. Think whether there was ever anything nearer to you, more familiar, more indispensable than such a thing. Whether everything else—except it—was not capable of acting unkindly or unjustly towards you, of frightening you with pain, or confusing you with uncertainty? If, amongst your early experiences, you knew kindness, confidence and the sense of not being alone—do you not owe it to that thing? The first time you shared your little heart, as one shares a piece of bread which must suffice for two, was it not with a thing?

Later, in the legends of the saints, you found a holy joyfulness, a blessed humility, a readiness to be all things, qualities which were already familiar to you because some small piece of wood had once shown you them all, assuming and illustrating them for you. That small, forgotten object, willing as it was to represent any and every thing, made you familiar with thousands of things by filling a thousand rôles, by being animal and tree, and king and child; and when it ceased to play its part, all these things were there. That something, worthless as it was, prepared the way for your first contacts with the world, introduced you to life and to people; and, more than that, its existence, its outward appearance, whatever it was, its final destruction or mysterious withdrawal from the scene caused you to know the whole of human experience, even to death itself.

You scarcely remember it, and you are seldom aware that you still need things which, like the things of your childhood, expect your confidence, your affection, your devotion. How does this happen? How does it come about at all that things are related to us? What is their history?

Things were made very early, with difficulty, after the pattern of natural things already existing; utensils and vessels were made, and it must have been a strange experience to see the made object as a recognized existence, with the same rights and the same reality as the thing already there. Something came into existence blindly, through the fierce throes of work, bearing upon it the marks of exposed and threatened life, still warm with it—but no sooner was it finished and put aside than it took its place amongst the other things, assumed their indifference, their quiet dignity, and looked on, as it were, from a distance and from out its own permanence with melancholy consent. This experience was so remarkable and so great that we can understand how things soon came to be made solely for its sake. For the earliest images were possibly nothing but practical applications of this experience, attempts to form out of the visible human and animal world something immortal and permanent, belonging to an order immediately above that world: a thing.

What kind of a thing? A beautiful thing? No. Who would have known what beauty was? A similar thing. A thing in which one recognized again what one liked, and what one feared, and what remained incomprehensible.

Do you remember such things? Perhaps there is one which for a long time seemed to you simply ridiculous. But one day you were struck by its urgency, the peculiar, almost desperate earnestness which all things possess; and did you not notice how a beauty such as you would not have thought possible came over this thing almost against its will?

If you have experienced such a moment, I would now call it to my aid. It is the moment which restores things to their real life. For no object can affect you if you do not allow it to surprise you with an unimagined beauty. Beauty is always something added to that which is already there, and what that something is we do not know.

The fact that there existed aesthetic opinion, which believed itself capable of understanding beauty, has misled you and has produced artists who considered their vocation to be the creating of beauty. And it has not yet become superfluous to repeat that beauty cannot be "made". No one has ever made beauty. One can only create kindly or sublime conditions for that which sometimes dwells amongst us, an altar and fruits and a flame. The other is not in our power. And the thing itself which goes forth indestructible from human hands is like Socrates' Eros, is a daemon, is something between a god and a man, not in itself beautiful, but expressing pure love of and pure longing for beauty.

And now imagine how completely this idea must transform everything when it dawns upon a creative artist. The artist, guided by this knowledge, has no need to think of beauty; he knows as little as anyone else wherein it consists. Directed by his urge towards the realization of purposes far beyond him, he only knows that there are certain conditions under which beauty may consent to come to the things he makes. And his vocation is to learn to know those conditions and to acquire the power of producing them.

But whoever studies these conditions thoroughly learns that they do not pass beyond the surface and nowhere penetrate within; that all that one can do is to produce a definitely self-contained surface which is in no part accidental, a surface which, like that of natural objects, is surrounded by the atmosphere from which it receives its shadows and its lights, simply this surface, nothing else. Dissociated from all big-sounding, pretentious and capricious phraseology, art suddenly appears to take its place in the sober and inconsiderable life of every day, amongst the crafts. For what does it mean, to produce a surface?

But let us for a moment consider whether everything before us, everything we observe, explain, and interpret, does not consist simply of surfaces? And what we call mind and spirit and love: are these things not only a slight change seen on the small surface of our neighbour's face? And must not the artist, who would give us these in plastic form, keep to the tangible element which is in keeping with his medium, to the form which he can lay hold of and imitate? And whoever had the power of seeing and producing all forms, would he not (almost unconsciously) give us all spiritual emotion? Everything that has ever been called longing or pain or bliss or which, by reason of its inexpressible spirituality, cannot even be given a name?

For all happiness that has ever thrilled the heart; all greatness, even to think of which almost destroys us; every spacious, world-transforming idea: there was a moment when these were nothing but a pursing of the lips, the lifting of the eyebrows or the shadow on a brow: and this contour of the mouth, this line above the eyelids, this shadow on a face—perhaps they have previously existed in exactly similar form: as a marking on an animal, a fissure in a rock, a hollow in a fruit . . .

There is only one single surface which suffers a thousand changes and transformations. It was possible to think of the whole world for a moment under this conception, so that it became simple, and was placed as a task to be accomplished in the hands of the man who so thought of it. For the endowment of an object with life of its own does not depend on great ideas but upon whether out of such ideas one can create a *métier*, a daily labour, something that remains with one to the end.

And now I venture to say to you the name which cannot be withheld any longer: Rodin. You know it is the name of countless objects. You ask to see them, and I am confused because I cannot show you any of them.

But I seem to see one and another in your memory, and feel as if I could lift them out and place them here in our midst:

    that man with the broken nose, unforgettable as a suddenly raised fist;

that youth, whose upward stretching is as near to you as your own awakening;

that walking figure, which stands like a new word for the action of walking in the vocabulary of your feeling;

and the man sitting, thinking with his whole body, withdrawing into himself;

and the burgher with the key, like some great receptacle containing only pain.

And Eve bending down as if from the distance into the embrace of her own arms, whose outward turning hands would ward off all things, even her own changing body.

And the sweet, soft, Inner Voice, armless as life within, and separated, like some member apart, from the rhythm of the group.

And some small thing whose name you have forgotten, made out of a white shining embrace which holds together like a knot; and that other thing, called, perhaps, Paolo and Francesca, and still smaller ones which you find within you like thin-skinned fruits—

and: now your eyes, like the lenses of a magic lantern, throw over and past me on to the wall a gigantic Balzac. The figure of a creator in his arrogance, erect in the midst of his own motion as in a vortex which catches the whole world up into this seething head.

And now that these things, taken from your memory, are present with us, shall I put beside them others from the many hundred things? That Orpheus, that Ugolino, that St. Theresa receiving the stigmata, that Victor Hugo with his commanding gesture, oblique and massive, and that other figure oblivious to all but the whispering voices, and still a third, to whom three maidens' voices from below are singing, like some source springing forth from the earth to greet him? And I feel the name vanishing in my mouth and feel that all this is simply the Poet, the same Poet who is called Orpheus when his arm, with a wide sweep embracing all things, is lifted to the strings, the same who, with convulsive anguish, clings to the feet of the fleeing Muse as she escapes; the same who, finally, dies, his face upright in the shadow of his voices which cease not to fill the world with song, and so dies that this little group is often known as *Resurrection*.

But who can keep back the surge of lovers which rises out beyond on the ocean of this man's work? With these figures relentlessly linked together there come destinies and sweet and comfortless names: but suddenly they vanish like a passing radiance—and we understand why. We see men and women, men and women, and again men and women. And the longer one looks, the more does even this content become simplified, and one sees: Things.

At this point my words lose their power of expression and revert to the great discovery for which I have already prepared you, the knowledge of the one surface, knowledge which placed the whole world at the disposal of this art. Placed it at its disposal, but did not yet bestow it. Infinite labour was necessary (is still necessary) before it could be appropriated.

Consider the labour entailed when the goal was to gain the mastery of all surfaces; for no one thing is like another. When the artists did not merely aim at knowing the body in general, the face, the hand (these things do not exist); but all bodies, all faces, all hands. What a task is this! And how simple and serious it is; devoid of fascination or promise; entirely unpretentious.

It implies a craft, but, as it seems, a craft for one who is more than mortal, so immense is it, so endless and without limit and so dependent upon a never-ceasing apprenticeship. And where was to be found a patience which should be equal to such a labour?

It was found in the love of this incessant worker, in which it was constantly renewed. For that is, perhaps, the secret of this master, namely, that he was a lover whom nothing could withstand. His desire was so lasting and passionate and uninterrupted that all things capitulated: the things of nature and the enigmatic things of all ages, in which human feeling sought to be a part of Nature. He was not satisfied with those which commanded ready admiration. He wanted to learn admiration in all its phases. He appropriated the difficult, reticent things, carrying them like a burden, the weight of which forced him further and further into his craft. Under their pressure it must have become clear to him that with objects of art, just as with a weapon or a balance, what matters is not the outward appearance and the "effect" thereby produced, but that far more important is good workmanship.

This quality of workmanship, this conscientiousness of execution, was everything. To reproduce a thing meant to have made oneself familiar with every part, to have hidden nothing, overlooked nothing, nowhere to have used deceit; to know all the hundred profiles, to be familiar with it from every angle, from above and from below. Only then did the thing exist, only then did it become an island separated on all sides from the continent of the uncertain.

This work (the work of the *modelé*) was the same in everything one made, and had to be carried out so humbly, so obediently, so devotedly, so impartially on face and hand and body that no specified parts remained and the artist worked at the form without knowing what exactly would result, like a worm working its way from point to point in the dark. For who remains uninfluenced when confronted with forms which have definite names? Who does not exercise power of selection when he calls something face? But the creative artist has no right to select. His work must be permeated by a spirit of unvarying obedience. The forms must pass through his fingers untampered with, like something entrusted to his keeping, if they are to appear pure and intact in his work.

And that the forms in Rodin's work are: pure and intact; without questioning he transmitted them to his works, which, when he leaves them, seem never to have known human touch. Light and shadow grow soft about them as about fresh fruit, and more alive with movement, as if brought hither by the morning wind.

Here we must speak of movement; not, indeed, in the sense in which it has so often been mentioned with reproach; for the mobility of the gestures, which has attracted much attention in this sculpture, takes place within the things, like the circulation of an inner current, never disturbing the architectural calm and stability. The introduction of movement into plastic art would have been nothing new. What is new is the kind of movement which light has been made to impart by means of the peculiar treatment of the surfaces, the inclines of which are so manifoldly varied that light flows from them now slowly, now in a cascade, appearing now shallow and now deep, gleaming or dull. The light which falls on one of these things is no longer any light, is no longer accidental in any of its effects; the thing takes possession of it and uses it as something of its own. This acquisition and appropriation of light, as the result of a quite clearly defined surface, was recognized by Rodin to be an essential characteristic of plastic objects. The antique and the Gothic had, each in its own way, sought a solution of this problem of plastic art, and he placed himself in line with the most ancient traditions when, at this stage in his development, he strove to master the problem of light.

There actually exist marbles which have their own light, such as the bowed countenance resting on the block in the Luxembourg Museum, *La Pensée*. It leans so far forward as to become shadowy, and the white shimmer of the marble above which it rests is such that under its influence the shadows melt and pass into a transparent *clair-obscur*. And who does not remember with delight one of the smaller groups in which two bodies create a twilight, in the veiled softness of which they meet? And is it not remarkable to see the light passing over the recumbent back of the Danaïde, slowly, as if the hours scarcely caused it to advance? And did anyone know of that complete gamut of shadows reaching to the shy transparent darkness which we see sometimes about the navel in certain small antiques, and which we now only find in the hollow of curved rose-leaves?

Such developments—difficult to express in words—mark the advance in Rodin's work. With the conquest of light began the next great achievement, to which his things owe their appearance of largeness, a largeness independent of all measurement. I refer to the conquest of space.

Once again things came to his aid, as so often before, things outside in nature and isolated things in art of noble origin, to which he returned constantly to question them. Their answer was invariably a conformity to law, with which they were filled and which he gradually came to understand. They revealed to him a mysterious geometry of space from which he learnt that if an object was really to take its place in space, to be recognized there, as it were, in its cosmic independence, its contours must be arranged in the direction of certain planes inclining towards each other.

It is difficult to express precisely what this knowledge was. But in Rodin's work we can see how he applied it. With ever increasing decisiveness and assurance the given details are brought together in strongly marked surface-units, until finally they adjust themselves, as if under the influence of rotating forces, in a number of great planes, and we get the impression that these planes are part of the universe and could be continued into infinity.

There is the *Youth of Primitive Times*, standing as if in an enclosed space; about *John* this space widens in all directions; *Balzac* is surrounded by the whole atmosphere, but a number of headless figures, in particular the tremendous new version of the *Man walking*, seem to pass into a sphere far beyond us, into infinite space, amongst the stars, into a vast, unerring rhythm of the spheres.

But as in a fairy-tale the gigantic, when once conquered, becomes small for the conqueror that it may become entirely his, so in the same way the master, once his works have appropriated space, was able to take possession of it for his own use. For we find it undiminished in all its vastness in those strange sheets, which ever and again cause one to think that they are the climax of his work. These drawings of the last ten years are not, as so many take them to be, rapid jottings, preparatory and transitory studies; they contain a final statement of long, uninterrupted experience. And this they contain, as by a miracle, in something which is nothing, in a rapid outline, in a contour breathlessly caught from Nature, in the contour of a contour too delicate and precious for Nature to retain. Never have lines, even in the rarest of Japanese drawings, possessed such a power of expression and at the same time been so innocent of purpose. For there is no representation here, no intention, no trace of a name. And withal what is not here? Is there any attitude of holding or of letting go or of no longer being able to hold, of bending and stretching and contracting, of falling or flying, ever seen or imagined, which is not found here? And if they ever occurred, they were lost; for they were so fleeting and fine, had so little reference to oneself, that it was not possible to give them a meaning. Now for the first time, seen unexpectedly in these sheets, the meaning becomes clear: the utmost we know of love and suffering, and bliss and woe, breathes from these sheets, we know not why. There are figures rising up, and their rising is as intoxicating as only a morning can be through which the sun breaks. And there are light, swiftly departing figures, whose departure fills us with dismay, as though we could not do without them. There are recumbent figures surrounded by sleep and piled up dreams; and languid figures heavy with languor, waiting; and forms of the depraved who cannot wait. We see their vice, like the growth of a plant, growing in sanity because it cannot do otherwise; we feel how much there is of the bending of a flower in the bending figure, and that all this is part of the world, even to this figure which, like a sign of the zodiac, is eternally remote and held fast in its own passionate solitude.

But when one of these animated figures is seen behind slightly green colour, we have the sea or the ocean bed, and the figure moves differently and with difficulty beneath the water; and a touch of blue behind a falling form suffices to bring all space tumbling into the picture on all sides and to develop the figure with so great a void that one is seized with dizziness and involuntarily clutches at the hand of the master who, with the delicate gesture of one offering a gift, is holding it out.

Now, I see, I have shown you one of the master's gestures. You ask for others. You feel sufficiently prepared to form a co-ordinated whole by adding outward and incidental features, as parts of the personal picture. You desire to hear the sound of a sentence, as it was spoken; you want to enter places and dates in the mountain and river map of this work.

There is a photograph taken from an oil-painting. It shows somewhat indistinctly a young man at the end of the sixties. The simple lines of the beardless face are almost hard, but the clear eyes looking out of the shadow give to the whole a mild, almost dreamy expression like that of young people who have known solitude; it is almost the face of one who has read until it is dark.

But there is another likeness, dating from 1880. In it is seen a man who bears the stamp of activity. The face has become thin, the long beard flows carelessly on to the broad-shouldered chest, over which the coat has grown too loose. One fancies one can see in the ashen, faded tones of the photograph that the eyelids are red, but the gaze of the tired eyes is resolute and confident, and the whole bearing expresses an elastic tension which will not fail.

And suddenly, within the course of a few years, all that seems to be changed. What was temporary and indeterminate has been replaced by what is definite and calculated to last. Suddenly we have this brow, "rocky" and steep, with the strong, straight nose, and the delicate, sensitive nostrils. The eyes, with the deep penetration of their inward and outward gaze, lie as if beneath ancient carved arches. The mouth of a faun's mask, half concealed and with the additional sensuous silence of new centuries, and beneath it the beard, as if too long restrained, cascading downward, in one single white billow. And the figure which carries this head apparently immovable.

And if one had to say what it is that emanates from this figure, it would be this: that it seems to reach back into far ages like a river-god, and to gaze into the future like a prophet. It bears no mark of our own time. Quite definite in its uniqueness, it yet loses itself in a certain mediaeval anonymity, it has that humility of greatness which recalls the builders of the great cathedrals. Its solitude is not aloofness, for it is in close association with Nature. Its virility, with all its firmness, is not hard; indeed, a friend of Rodin's, whom he used to visit in the evenings, could write, "When he goes, he leaves behind him some quality of gentleness in the twilight of the room, as if a woman had been there."

And, in fact, those accepted into the friendship of the master know his kindness, which is elemental like the kindness of a natural force, like the kindness of a long summer day which causes all things to grow and does not end till late. But even the passing visitors of the Saturday afternoons had a share of it when they met the master in the two town studios in the *Dépôt des Marbres* amongst completed and half-finished works. From the very first moment his courtesy gave one a feeling of security, but the intensity of his interest was almost terrifying when directed towards one. For then he had that concentrated gaze which comes and goes like the light of a lighthouse, but which is so strong that one can feel its bright reflection far behind one.

You have often heard these workshops in the Rue de l'Université described. They are sheds in which the blocks are hewn for this great work. Inhospitable as quarries almost, they offer no diversion to the visitor; designed solely for work, they compel him to set about the work of seeing, and many have felt in this place for the first time how unfamiliar that work is to them. Those who learnt it went forth with a new acquirement, and everything outside made them aware that they had learnt. But without doubt these rooms were most remarkable of all for those who could see. Guided by a sense of gentle necessity, they came, often from a distance, and felt that to stand here under the protection of these things was something which was destined to happen at some time in their lives. It was a completion and a beginning and the quiet fulfilment of the wish that somewhere there should be an example in the midst of many words, the simple reality of achievement. Such visitors Rodin approached, and admired with them what they admired. For his instinctive method of work, without intention, involving simply a craft, makes it possible for him, once they are there, to stand in admiration before his own completed works, over which he has exercised neither guardianship nor tutelage. And his admiration is always better, more thorough and more filled with delight than that of the visitor. He has the advantage of his indescribable power of concentration. And when in conversation he tolerantly, with an ironical smile, repudiates the imputation of inspiration and expresses the opinion that there is no such thing—no inspiration, but only work, one suddenly comprehends that for this creative artist inspiration has become permanent, that he no longer feels its approach because it is never absent, and one guesses the reason of his uninterrupted fertility.

"Have you worked well?" is the question with which he greets anyone he is fond of; for, if it can be answered in the affirmative, there is nothing more to ask and one can rest satisfied: he who works, is happy.

Rodin's simple and undivided nature, with its incredible resources of energy, made this solution possible; his genius made it a necessity; only in such a way could it take possession of the world. His destiny was to work as Nature works, not as men.

It is possible that Sebastian Melmoth felt this when, solitary, he set forth on one of those sad afternoons of his to view the *Porte de l'Enfer*. It is possible that the hope of making a new beginning flickered once again in his half-crushed heart. Perhaps, if it had been possible, he would have liked to ask this man, when he was alone with him, "What was your life like?" And Rodin would have answered, "Good."

"Had you any enemies?"

"They were not able to prevent me from working."

"And Fame?"

"Made work a duty."

"And your friends?"

"Expected work from me."

"And women?"

"My work taught me to admire them."

"But you have been young?"

"Then I was like any other. When one is young, one has no understanding; that comes later, by degrees."

What Sebastian Melmoth left unasked has perhaps been in the minds of many, looking repeatedly at the master, amazed by the undiminished power of his almost seventy years, by his youthfulness, which is as fresh and unpreserved as if it were constantly flowing forth to him from the earth.

And you yourselves ask again impatiently, "What was his life like?"

If I hesitate to give it to you chronologically, as is usual in describing a life, it is because all the dates we know (and they are very isolated) seem to be so impersonal and general when compared with what this man made of them. The impassable mountain range of his mighty work, blocking the way to all that went before, makes it difficult for us to recognize the past; our only source of information is what the master himself has related and what others have repeated.

Of his childhood we know only that he was early sent from Paris to a small pension in Beauvais, where he missed his home and, being delicate and sensitive, suffered amongst those who made him feel strange and treated him harshly. He returned to Paris at the age of fourteen and learnt to work with clay in a little drawing-school, and so greatly did this material appeal to him that he was happiest with it in his hands. Indeed, anything in the way of work gave him pleasure: he worked even during meals, reading or drawing. He drew as he went along the street, and quite early in the morning he drew the sleepy animals in the *Jardin des Plantes*. And when love of work failed, poverty drove him to it. Poverty, without which his life would be unthinkable. He never forgets that it made him one with the beasts and flowers, devoid of possessions amongst those who have nothing, who depend on God and on Him alone.

At the age of seventeen he entered the service of a decorator and worked for him as he later worked for Carrier-Belleuse in the factory at Sèvres and for van Rasbourg in Antwerp and in Brussels. His own independent life began, as far as the public was concerned, about 1877. It began with the accusation that he had made the statue of the *Âge d'airain*, exhibited at this time, by taking a cast from Nature. It began with an accusation. He would probably have forgotten about it by now if public opinion had not persisted, as it has, in accusing and rejecting him. He does not complain; but, as the result of constant hostility, he has developed a good memory for unpleasant experiences, which he would otherwise, with his feeling for essentials, have allowed to fall into disuse. His powers were already tremendous at this period, even as early as 1864, when he created the mask of the *Man with the Broken Nose*. He had done a great deal when working for others, but it had been marred by other hands and did not bear his name. The models which he made for Sèvres were found later by Mr. Roger-Marx and acquired by him; they had been thrown as useless amongst the broken fragments in the factory. Ten masks, designed for one of the fountains of the Trocadéro, vanished from their place as soon as they were put in position and have never been found again. The *Burghers of Calais* were refused the site which the master had suggested; nobody would take part in the unveiling of that statue. In Nancy Rodin was forced to make alterations, running counter to his own judgment, in the socle of the statue of Claude Lorrain. You will still remember the unheard of rejection of the *Balzac* by those who gave the commission, on the ground that the statue did not sufficiently resemble the original. Perhaps you failed to notice in the newspapers that, about two years ago, the plaster cast of the *Thinker*, put up outside the Panthéon to try the effect, was destroyed by blows of an axe. But a like announcement may meet your eye even to-day or to-morrow, if one of Rodin's works should be bought from public funds. For we can scarcely expect that this list of insults, containing only a few of those assiduously offered to him, is finally closed.

It is conceivable that an artist might, in the end, have joined issue in a warfare so constantly declared against him; that anger and impatience might have got the better of him; but how greatly it would have estranged him from his work so to enter the lists. It is Rodin's victory that he kept to his work and responded to destructive forces in Nature's way, namely, by beginning afresh with tenfold fertility.

He who fears the reproach of exaggeration is powerless to describe Rodin's activity after his return from Belgium. His day began with the sun but did not end with it; for a long spell of lamplight was added to the many hours of daylight. Late at night, too late for any model, his wife, who had long shared his life with touching devotion and helpfulness, was ever ready to make work possible in his shabby room. She was an unobtrusive helpmeet, concealed behind the many menial duties which fell to her lot, but the bust called *La Bellone* does not allow us to forget that she could be beautiful and the portrait of a later date shows it too. When at last she grew tired, the artist did not need to interrupt his work, because his mind was so stored with form memories.

At this period were laid the foundations of his whole immeasurable output; nearly all the pieces known to us began at this time with an astonishing simultaneousness. As if the only pledge of the possibility of carrying out such tremendous undertakings was to begin their realization. And for years on end this immense power continued undiminished, and when, finally, a certain exhaustion made itself felt, the cause was not work but rather the unhealthy conditions of the sunless dwelling (in the Rue des Grands-Augustins), which Rodin had long disregarded. No doubt he had often felt the want of Nature, and Sunday afternoons were frequently spent out of doors; but evening had generally fallen when, as one amongst the many on foot (for years there was no question of taking an omnibus), he reached the fortifications, beyond which lay the country, indistinct and unattainable in the twilight. But at last it became possible to realize his long cherished desire and to move right into the country; at first to the little country house at Bellevue, once inhabited by Scribe, and later to the heights of Meudon.

There life became much more spacious; the house (the one-storied Villa des Brillants with the steep Louis XIII roof) was small and has not since been enlarged. But now there was a garden which, with its cheerful activity, shared in all that took place, and distance lay before the windows. In these new surroundings it was not the master of the house who took up room and claimed constant extensions, it was his beloved works, which were now to be indulged. For them everything was done;

six years ago—you will remember—he transferred the Exhibition Pavilion from the Pont d'Alma to Meudon and gave up that bright and lofty room to these things which now fill it in their hundreds.

Beside this *Musée Rodin* has grown up gradually a museum of classic statues and fragments, selected personally with much thought and care. It contains works by Greek and Egyptian artists, some of which would be remarkable even in the rooms of the Louvre. In another room there are pictures behind Attic vases, the painters of which one can name without looking for the signatures: Ribot, Monet, Carrière, van Gogh, Zuloaga, and, amongst those that cannot be named, there are some who trace their descent from Falguière, who was a great painter. As is natural, there are many dedications: the books alone form a numerous library, a library curiously independent of its owner and his choice, and yet by no means fortuitously brought together. All these things are surrounded by care and held in honour, but no one expects them to contribute amenity or atmosphere. One has almost the sensation of never having felt so strongly the undiminished individual effect of works of art of the most different kinds and periods as in this place, where they have no appearance of striving to please as in a collection, and are not forced to contribute of their own store of beauty to a general sense of well-being which has no reference to them. Someone said once that they were kept like beautiful animals, and that really does describe Rodin's relationship to the things about him; when he moves about amongst them, often at night, cautiously as if not to awaken them, and finally goes up, with a small light in his hand, to a piece of antique marble, which stirs, awakens, and suddenly arises from its sleep, it is Life which he is seeking and which he now reverently admires: "La vie, cette merveille," as he once wrote.

Here, in the solitude of his country dwelling, he has learnt to embrace this Life with still greater faith and love. It reveals itself to him now as to one of the initiated, it no longer hides itself from him, it has no distrust towards him. He recognizes it in what is small and in what is great; in what is scarcely discernible and in what is immense. It is present in his rising up and in his going to rest and in the night watches; the simple old-fashioned repasts are filled with it, the bread and the wine; it is in the joy of a dog, it is in the swans and in the shining flight of doves. It is present in all its fullness in every tiny flower and is a hundredfold in every fruit. Any cabbage leaf from the kitchen garden makes proud display of it, and rightly so. How it delights to shine in the water and how happy it is in the trees! And how eagerly it invades the existence of men, when no barriers are set up against it. How pleasantly the little houses over there stand in the right kind of plains, just as they should. And with what splendid rhythm the bridge at Sèvres leaps across the river, pausing, resting, gathering strength and leaping forward again three times. And away in the distance behind it, Mont-Valérien with its fortresses, like a great monument, like an Acropolis, like a Greek altar. And these things here have also been made by men familiar with life: this Apollo, this Buddha resting on the open flower, this hawk, and here this lean torso of a boy, in which nothing is untrue. Upon such foundations, constantly confirmed by things near and far, rest the working days of the master of Meudon. Working days they remain, all alike, only that now part of the work consists in this outward gaze, this sharing the life of all things, this understanding. "Je commence à comprendre"—he often says, thoughtfully and thankfully. "And this is because I have devoted myself seriously to something; he who understands one thing, understands all; for the same laws are in all. I learnt sculpture and I knew very well that it was something great. I remember now that in the *Imitation of Christ*, particularly in the third book, I once put sculpture everywhere in place of God, and it was right and gave the right meaning——"

You smile, and it is quite right to smile at this saying; its deeper meaning is so unprotected that one feels one must conceal it. But you notice that words like these are not meant to be spoken as loudly as I have to speak here. Their mission is, perhaps, fulfilled, when individuals, receiving them personally, endeavour to shape their lives accordingly.

For the rest, Rodin is silent like all men of action. He seldom allows himself the right of applying his knowledge in words, because that belongs to the poet; and, in his modesty, he places the poet far above the sculptor, who has "to exert himself indescribably to understand the Muse, so dull is he," as he once remarked, with a smile of renunciation, before his lovely group *Le sculpteur et sa muse.*

Nevertheless, what has been said of his talk holds good: "Quelle impression de bon repas, de nourriture enrichissante ———"; for behind every word of his conversation stands, massive and reassuring, the simple reality of his days filled with experience.

You can understand now that these days are full. The forenoon is spent in Meudon; often several works already begun, in the different studios, are resumed in turn and carried forward a little; into the midst of this business affairs obtrude themselves, troublesome and unavoidable, for, since scarcely any of his creations pass through the art dealer's hands, the master is not spared that worry and work.

By two o'clock there is generally a model waiting for him in the town, someone sitting for a portrait or a professional model; and it is only in summer that Rodin succeeds in getting back to Meudon before nightfall. The evening out there is short and never varies, for regularly at nine o'clock the household retires.

And you ask about diversions, about exceptions; there are none really; the truth of Renan's "travailler, ça repose" has perhaps never been shown as it is shown here daily. But Nature sometimes quite unexpectedly enlarges these days, which outwardly are so alike, adding seasons, whole holidays, before the day begins; she does not allow her friend to miss anything. Mornings shining with happiness awaken him and he shares their life. He watches his garden or goes to Versailles to attend the resplendent awakening of the Park, as one went to the levée of the King. He loves the virginity of these first hours. "On voit les animaux et les arbres chez eux," he says cheerfully, and notices everything that stands rejoicing by the wayside. He takes up a mushroom with delight and shows it to Madame Rodin who, like himself, has not given up these early walks. "Look," he says excitedly. "And that takes only a night; it is made in one night, all these lamellae. That is good work."

At the edge of the park the rural landscape lies spread out. A yoke of four oxen ploughing turns slowly, moving ponderously in the fresh field. Rodin admires the slow movement, its unhurried deliberateness, its ample sufficiency. And then he speaks, "It is all obedience." In like manner his thoughts move through the work. He understands this picture, as he understands the pictures of the poets, with whom he sometimes of an evening occupies himself (no longer with Baudelaire, now and again with Rousseau, very often with Plato). But then, when horns sound, quick and tumultuous, from the drill-ground of St. Cyr across the peaceful labour of the land—he smiles: he sees the shield of Achilles.

And at the next turning the high road lies before him, "la belle route", level and long, eloquent of walking. And walking too is a joy. His Belgian days taught him that. Very skilful at his work, and his time being, for various reasons, only half occupied by the colleague for whom he then worked, he gained whole days which he spent in the country. It is true he took a paint box with him, but used it less and less, because he saw that when he occupied himself with some one particular he lost the joy of a thousand other things which he as yet knew so little. And so it was a time of looking at things. Rodin calls it his richest time. The great beech-woods of Soignes, the long, shining highways, running out from them to meet the far-blowing wind of the plains, the bright inns in which rest and food had something festive about them, for all their simplicity (it was mostly bread dipped in wine, "une trempête"): this was for long the world of his impressions, into which each simple event entered as if accompanied by an angel; for behind each he recognized the wings of some glory.

He is undoubtedly right to think of these years of walking and gazing with peculiar gratitude. They were his preparation for the coming work; in every sense the necessary preliminary, for it was then also that his health was so permanently established that he was able later to make ruthless demands upon it.

Just as he brought inexhaustible vitality with him out of those years, so now he returns from a long morning walk refreshed and eager for work. Happy as if he had received good news, he enters the room in which his things are and goes up to one of them as if he had brought something lovely for it. And the next moment he is absorbed, as if he had been working for hours. Now he begins one thing, completes another, modifies another, as if responding to their call as he passes through their midst and sees their need of him. He forgets none of them; those in the background bide their time and are in no hurry. Neither in a garden does everything grow at the same time. Blossoms are found beside fruit, and here and there a tree is only in leaf. Have I not said that it is an essential characteristic of this mighty genius to have as much time as Nature and to produce like her?

I repeat it, and it still remains a miracle to me, that there is such a man whose work has assumed such proportions. But I cannot forget the look of alarm which checked me once when, in a small company of people, I used those words in order to call up for a moment the whole immensity of Rodin's genius. One day I understood that look.

I was passing through the vast workshops, lost in thought, and I noticed that everything was in a state of growth and that nothing was in a hurry. There stood the *Thinker*, in bronze, mightily concentrated within himself, completed; but he was part of the still growing complexity of the *Gate of Hell*. There was one of the monuments of Victor Hugo, advancing slowly towards completion, still under observation, still liable perhaps to alteration, and further off stood the other versions still incomplete. There lay the Ugolino group, like the unearthed roots of an ancient oak, waiting. There was waiting the remarkable monument for Puvis de Chavannes with the table, the apple-tree, and the glorious spirit of eternal peace. And over yonder was what I took to be a monument for Whistler, and this recumbent figure here will, perhaps, some day make famous the grave of some unknown person. One can scarcely make one's way through it all, but finally I arrived back at the small plaster cast of the *Tour de Travail*, which, now that its design has reached its final form, only awaits a patron who will help to set up the immense lesson of its imagery in the midst of men.

But here beside me is another work, a quiet face to which belongs a hand expressive of suffering, and the plaster has that transparent whiteness which only Rodin's instrument can impart. On the stand has been written, and already crossed out, the provisional legend: *Convalescente*. And now I find myself amongst objects all of which are new and nameless and still in the process of growth; they were begun yesterday or the day before or years ago; but they show the same unconcern as the others. They keep no count of time.

And then I asked myself for the first time: how is it possible that they are indifferent to time? Why is this immense work continually growing and where will it end? Does it think no more of its master? Does it really believe itself to be in the hands of Nature, like the rocks over which a thousand years pass as one day?

And it seemed to me in my amazement that all the finished works would have to be cleared out of the workshops, so that what remained to be done in the ensuing years might be seen. But while I was counting the many finished works, the shimmering stones, the bronzes, all these busts, my eye was caught by the lofty *Balzac*, which had returned to the studio, rejected, and now stood there proudly, as if refusing to leave it again.

And since that day I see the tragedy of the immensity of this work. I feel more clearly than ever before that in these works sculpture has developed continuously to such power as has not been known since the ancients. But this plastic art has been born into an age which possesses no things, no houses, no external objects. For the inner life of which this age consists is still without form, intangible: it is fluid.

This man had to lay hold of it; he was at heart a giver of form. He has seized upon all that was vague, ever-changing, developing, which was also within himself, and enclosed it in form and set it up like a god; for change has its god also. As if one had stopped the flow of molten metal and let it harden in one's hand.

Perhaps the opposition which his work everywhere encountered is, in part, explained by his use of force. Genius is always a cause of alarm to its own age; but here, where genius outstrips our age not merely in things spiritual but also in its powers of concrete realization, its effect is terrible, like a sign in the heavens.

One might almost be persuaded that there is nowhere any place for these things. Who will venture to receive them? And are they not themselves the confession of their own tragedy, these radiant things which, in their loneliness, have drawn the heavens about them? And which now stand there beyond the power of any building to control? They stand in space. What have they to do with us?

Imagine a mountain rising up within an encampment of nomads. They would leave it and depart on account of their flocks. And we are a nomad people, all of us; not because we have, individually, no home, beside which we stay and at which we work, but because we have no longer a common home. Because we must always carry what we have of greatness about with us, instead of setting it up from time to time where greatness is.

And yet, wherever there is real human greatness, it desires to shelter within universal nameless greatness. When once again, after the ancients, greatness at last burst forth from men in sculptured figures, from men who were also nomads in spirit and filled with change—how it flung itself upon the cathedrals, taking refuge in the vestibules and climbing doorways and towers, as at a time of inundation.

But where are Rodin's things to go?

Eugène Carrière once wrote of him, "Il n'a pas pu collaborer à la cathédrale absente." There was no place where he could collaborate and nobody worked with him.

In the houses of the eighteenth century and in its well-ordered parks he saw sorrowfully the last outward appearance of the inner life of an age. And patiently he discovered in it the marks of that union with nature which has since been lost. With ever increasing insistence he drew attention to it, counselling us to return "à l'œuvre même de Dieu, œuvre immortelle et redevenue inconnue". And he was referring to those who would come after him when, looking at the landscape, he said: "Voilà tous les styles futurs."

His works could not wait; they had to be made. He long foresaw their homelessness. The only choice he had was to destroy them while yet within him, or to win for them the sky which is about the mountains.

And that was his work.

He raised the immense arc of his world above us and made it a part of Nature.

Note to page 67

(1907)

(THE TOWER OF WORK)

REPEATED inquiries lead me to believe that a brief description of *The Tower of Work* may not seem superfluous. I base myself on the plaster model mentioned, which can be seen at the Musée Rodin in Meudon.

From a fairly spacious rectangular substructure there rises a circular tower. Its open arcades are momentarily reminiscent of the campanile in Pisa; yet the arches here do not stand in storeys one upon another; they wind upwards as a spiral band and are held together at the top by the girdle of a sculptured cornice. The whole terminates in a group of two winged figures resting on the platform enclosed by the cornice.

The substructure will contain a windowless rectangular hall, a kind of crypt, from whose walls, in bas-relief, representations of underground and undersea work, miners and divers, are to stand out under electric illumination. In front of the slightly recessed entrance to that room, on both sides, towering above the lower level, stand statues of Day and Night, architecturally fitted into the staircase leading up to the terrace of the substructure. From there the tower is entered. This consists of a massive column, along which, rising gently, the spiral staircase leads, enclosed on the outside by the arcades. Through these ample light falls upon the reliefs facing them; these, enlivening the surface of the column, accompany the stairs all the way up. Craft unrolls from craft, carpenters, bricklayers, blacksmiths – trade from trade, as if swept along and upwards by one gigantic movement. The band which finally ties the spiral at its end from outside bears the signs of the zodiac, intended to restate what the statues of Day and Night at the foot of the monument had already suggested: that all this is ceaselessly at work and rising upwards, towards the genii which, descending from the heavens with blessings, are attracted by the plenitude of active forces as if appealed to.

At the base of the tower there are two more stone reliefs, like epitaphs, set in the wall, reminiscent of Hercules and Hephaestus, the heroic forebears of human labour.

The other figures represented wear the dress of our age; the style of the building, in its totality and in detail (arcades, doors, etc.), follows the forms of the French Renaissance.

(1913) For this great project is now little hope of realization, partly because the trends within the œuvre have taken other directions, partly because the decisive commission has failed to materialize; if this had come at the right moment it would have tipped the scales.

(1919) It probably was not Rodin's death which prevented the implementation of this great project. The lack of clients commissioning it and of like-minded collaborators did not favour its realization from the outset. The *Gates of Hell*, on the other hand, this greatest mountain range of his creation, the work which for decades served the master as a quarry of ideas, now, in a new composition arranged by him before his death, seems to be waiting for the bronze. The *Whistler Monument* is said to be ready for casting, the upright *Victor Hugo* intended for the Panthéon awaits its translation into marble, and the memorial for *Puvis de Chavannes* is reported to have been completed with the collaboration of Despiau. The long string of portraits is continued in three remarkable works: the bust of *Clemenceau*, started as early as 1913, the *Portrait of the Pope* of 1915 and the portrait of the Minister of Trade, *Clémentel*, Rodin's last work.

With Rodin's death the state has come into an enormous inheritance: the fine Hôtel de Biron, now the Musée Rodin, contains his entire artistic estate, including the rich collections. Through this institution even the fragmentary posthumous works are permanently assured of a link with his surviving œuvre.

Notes

(I)
(17 NOVEMBER 1900)

RODIN: This is what makes his sculpture so isolated, so much a fortress-like work of art: protecting itself, militant, inaccessible, attainable by a miracle only to those who feel they have wings: that it has liberated itself in the main from dependence on surroundings and background, that it has halted before its own stone, as if hesitating, upon the lips of the mountain range that has begun to tell its tale. (One recalls similar effects: in the region of Upper Italy, where Karst and Apennine grow together, a pine will sometimes stand on the edge of a bare rock, slender, praying with out-flung arms.) As a delicate and fragrant fruit with the whole aroma of its flesh, still warm from hidden summers, loosens itself from its shell, so these animated figures emerge from the hard stone. Like a thought from the massive brow which thought it, like a loved woman from a dark gloomy house in which much that is confused is heaped up: childhood of parents and ancestors, fear of the hour of death, small happinesses which seem to surface time and again from the dim smile of old mirrors, and the mournful note of songs started but, overcome by weeping, never played out: all these remain behind it, pressed together into a vague lump whose weight nearly crushes the rammed windows, and it steps forward, bright and lissom, and everything past seems to have happened only so at this moment to emphasize with its darkness the melancholy contours of its beautiful body. Parted from the stone from which they excavated themselves all works of sculpture used to stand homeless and orphaned, at the mercy of accidental surroundings, dependent on the wall that was slid behind them, pierced by light under bent arms and raised knees, not leaning against anything and not related to anything close; Rodin's sculptures, however, remain within all the intimacy of their native soil, in a hundred relationships with the stone, their great, gigantic past. They are infinitely aristocratic with the millennia behind them, to which they are linked by close kinship, and yet so largely in the spirit of an age which disdains talk of 'heroes', never producing the effect of exaggeration by an individual but instead fragments of great contexts and relationships, where each link has its specific role assigned to it. (Even in the monument of Honoré de Balzac, that magnificent figure in its indescribable pride does not seem like the representation of a hero. The tornado of imagination and will swirls up the column of the cloak upon whose foam-crested edge the intellectual head is set, as though moved by the delicate and delicious arbitrariness of that creative whirlwind.) Drama and sculpture share an endeavour not to present a hero around whom action and figures would rally, but so to represent movement and figures that they would allow the great centre to which they refer (but which always lies outside their orbit) to be surmised. Hauptmann's *Weavers*, Meunier's *Monument of Labour*, Bartholomé's *Tomb* and Rodin's *Burghers of Calais* are related in that sense. And it is a good thing for drama and sculpture occasionally to focus on each other. Parallels favour them, more so than any other two art forms. Both should be simple and have long-range effect. This is by the way.

   For sculpture there is one other circumstance that is exceedingly important: that the work of art should end within itself. Any 'looking-out-of-the-picture' can never arise inasmuch as a picture must always be extended in front of the figure concerned (foreground), to the same extent as behind it, so that the gaze of the figure invariably remains *within* the picture and is separated from the viewer as if by a non-conductive vacuum. A sculpture, which shares the same atmosphere with the viewer, must be better at 'looking away'. This means: it must be totally occupied with itself. This, too, Rodin has achieved to perfection: in his groups the eyes always gaze in relation to one another, there are no eyes, either in individual figures or in groups, which are not effective, i.e. confined, within each work. No viewer (not even the most conceited) will be able to claim that a bust by Rodin, say *Rochefort* or *Falguière*, let alone the inspired *Balzac*, has looked at him!

NOTES

(II)

(2 DECEMBER 1900)

On sculptures. There are sculptures which carry the environment in which they are imagined, or out of which they are raised, *within* themselves, they have absorbed it and they radiate it. The room in which a statue stands is its foreign land – it has its environment *within* itself, and its eye and the expression of its face relate to that environment concealed and folded within its shape. There are figures which radiate tightness, crowdedness, interior, and others which are undoubtedly imagined and seen in a wide open space, in a plain, against the sky. To him who sees them correctly it is always their Own-ness that is their native setting, not the accidental room in which they are placed or the empty wall against which they stand out.

Sculptures which have no milieu within them do indeed stand among the people, not encircled by any sacred ring and in no way different from objects of daily use – they are paperweights even if they are a thousand times larger than life and more.

(III)

(AUTUMN 1902, PARIS)

It is very beautiful to see him working. The connection between his eye and the clay. One believes one can see all the paths of his gaze, those sure, quick ones, forming a web in the air in which the thing gets increasingly entrapped. And how everything then becomes one: he and the thing, his thing; it would almost be impossible to tell which is the work.

... And when he speaks his voice sounds as if it were coming from within a tower, and his face is raised all dripping, as if from rushing water.

Description of Three Sculptures by Rodin

(c. 1905)

(I)
YOUNG GIRL CONFIDING HER SECRET TO ISIS OR TO NATURE

THIS group consists of two figures which, softly united, combine into an integrated intimity.

Confused by feelings and desires which did not exist in childhood, the young girl has sought refuge with this mature and severe woman who, kneeling and supported on her extended arms, makes no movement to accept her. One might regard her as totally indifferent had she not allowed the young girl, in the confused violence of her embrace, to draw her massive head down to her. Her face, bowed into the shadows, and its inflexible features seem to be illumined by the clear nudity of the girl, but they nevertheless remain as motionless as her body in its ancient mysterious attitude of the sphinx. The veil, flowing down from the goddess's head and back, piles up heavily on her lap, concealing the mystery of its prodigal and unconcerned fertility. Shivering with deep astonishment the young girl presses the buds of her breasts against the boundlessly maternal breast of the woman. With the whole of her youthful plant-like body she twists upwards and hides her face, while her mouth, invisible, pours out its secret, like a small spring, into this ocean of all eternal riddles.

(II)
CHRIST AND MARY MAGDALEN

Christ, in the gesture of the Crucifixion, his outstretched arms resembling a signpost at the crossroads of all pain, dies under the burden of his destiny which, like this stone (a heavy and petrified Cross), towers above him.

And she, who once came to anoint his indefatigable feet,

approaches, now that the sacrifice is accomplished, to surround this abandoned bloodless body with the belated and meaningless tenderness of her own. In a fit of despair she has thrown herself down on her knees before him. With her left arm she supports his abused head, whose expression she could not bear. And this face drifts along on her trembling arm, like a floating object, which she, bent over to the right, like a flame tormented by the wind, tries to embed and hide the ineffable suffering of this so greatly loved body in her own broken love. She surrounds him with a disconsolate and entreating movement, and with a gesture of hopelessness she loses her hair in order to bury Christ's tormented heart in it.

The marble clearly shows the contrast between the two bodies, and the contrast alone radiates the immeasurable sorrow immanent in the subject.

(III)

THE RUINS OF ATHENS

The city of Athens once upon a time lived like a beautiful woman. The fame of her beauty attracted the admiring glances of the world. Now she exists no more. Her body, which stood erect, like the Acropolis, has, now that it lies prone, become a mountain range whose outlines, with the light playing over them, vibrate in doleful lines, lamenting. Thus she is fast asleep; her sweet face, blossoming with distant memories, rests on her right hand, her left arm is lost in her loosed hair. And with her body and her sleep she encompasses a radiant past, the ruins of divine sculptures, the feet of heroes, the breasts of goddesses, the heads of ephebes and the flora of capitals in which, blissfully, the sap still teems.

And from the base of this mountain range young flowers ascend in multitudes, as though to seek their vanished sisters from the past.

This marble, whose surface is alive with the most delicate transitions, breathes an atmosphere as though of descending night, filled with the sweet sadness of the Moon.

Concerning Landscape

WE know so little about the painting of Antiquity; but it is safe to assume that it saw people as later painters have seen landscape. In the scenes of their vases, those unforgettable memorials of a great art of drawing, the surroundings (house or street) are only mentioned, as it were in abbreviated form, only indicated by their initial, but the naked human beings are everything, they are like trees bearing fruit and wreaths of fruit, and like shrubs in blossom, and like springs in which the birds are singing. In that age the body, which was cultivated like a piece of land, tended carefully like a harvest, and which one owned as one owns a valuable property, was the thing looked upon, was beauty, was the image through which all meanings passed in rhythmic movements, gods and animals, and all life's senses. Man, although he had existed for thousands of years, was too new to himself, too delighted with himself, to look beyond or away from himself. The landscape was the road on which he walked, the course which he covered, it was all the places of sport and dance where the Grecian day was spent; the valleys in which the armies assembled, the harbours from which one set forth on adventure and to which one returned full of unheard-of memories and older; the days of festival and the garlanded silver-sounding nights which followed, the processions to the gods and the encircling of the altar: that was the landscape in which he lived. But the mountain, on which no gods in human likeness dwelt, was foreign, the foot-hills where no statue, visible from afar, was to be seen, the slopes untrodden by any shepherd—these were undeserving of mention. All was but a stage and empty so long as man did not appear to fill the scene with the cheerful or tragic action of his body. Everything awaited him and, when he came, everything withdrew to give him room.

Christian art lost this connexion with the body, without gaining thereby any real approach to landscape; in it men and things were like letters and it formed long, painted sentences with an alphabet of initials. Human beings were garments, and bodies only in hell; and the landscape was rarely the earth. It was almost always made to represent heaven when it was pleasing, and when it aroused terror and was wild and inhospitable, it stood for the place of the damned and the eternally lost. It was already seen; for human beings had become attenuated and transparent, but it was natural for Christian art to feel landscape as a slight, transitory thing, as a strip of green overgrown graves beneath which hung hell and above which the great heavens opened as the actual, deep reality, desired of all Being. Now that there were three regions, three dwelling-places, which were much talked of: heaven, earth, and hell—a definite indication of the region became urgently necessary. It had to be seen and depicted; in the early Italian masters this depiction developed to great perfection, beyond its immediate purpose, and one has only to recall the paintings in Campo Santo at Pisa to feel that the idea of landscape for its own sake had by this time definitely emerged. It is true, they thought to indicate a region and nothing more, but they did this with such warmth of feeling and devotion, they told of the things attached to the earth, to the despised earth, denied by man, with such moving eloquence, revealing so much love: that this kind of painting seems to us to-day like a song in praise of earth, in which the saints join. And all the things seen were new, so that constant wonder was mingled with the beholding of them and joy over endless discoveries. Thus it followed naturally that they praised high heaven together with the earth and became familiar with it, for their whole longing was to know it. For a deep piety is like the rain: it always falls back again on to the earth, whence it came, and brings blessing to the fields.

Without intending to, they had so felt the warmth, the happiness, and the glory which can radiate from a meadow, a stream, a flower-covered slope and from trees standing fruit-laden, the one beside the other, that when they painted Madonnas, they surrounded them with this wealth as with a mantel, crowned them with it as with a crown and unfurled landscape like a banner in praise of them; for they knew not how to prepare for them any more ecstatic festival, they knew no offering comparable to this: to bring to them all the newly-found beauty and make it part of them. They no longer indicated any region by it, not even heaven, their landscape broke into song like a hymn to Mary, the music of which sounded in clear, bright colours.

But therewith a great development had taken place: the painter depicted landscape, and yet in doing so was not concerned with *it* but with himself; it had become the pretext for human emotion, a symbol of human joy, simplicity, and piety. It had become art. And Leonardo took it over in this form. The landscapes in his pictures are the expression of his deepest experience and knowledge, blue mirrors, in which hidden laws reflectingly behold themselves, distances large like the future and like it unfathomable. It is no accident that Leonardo, who was the first to paint people as experiences, as destinies which he had explored alone, felt landscape to be a medium of expression for almost inexpressible experience, depth, and sadness. To this man, who overtook many yet to come, it was given to use all the arts in a manner infinitely great; he spoke in them, as if in a variety of languages, of his life and of his life's discoveries and distant vistas.

No one has painted a landscape which is so entirely landscape and yet so much confession and the painter's own voice as is the depth of background behind the Madonna Lisa. It is as if all that is human were present in her infinitely quiet portrait, but as if everything else, all in front of man and beyond him, were in this mysterious complex of hills, trees, bridges, sky, and water. This landscape is not the picture of an impression, not a man's view of quiescent things; it is Nature which came into existence, a world which grew and was as foreign to man as the untrodden forest of an undiscovered island. To see landscape thus, as something distant and foreign, something remote and without allure, something entirely self-contained, was essential, if it was ever to be a medium and an inspiration for an autonomous art; for it had to be distant and very different from us, if it was to be capable of becoming a redemptive symbol for our destiny. It had to be almost hostile in its sublime indifference, if it was to give a new meaning to our existence with its things.

And it was in this sense that that art of landscape developed, which Leonardo da Vinci anticipated. It developed slowly throughout the centuries in the hands of isolated artists. The way to be traversed was very long, for it was difficult to wean oneself from the world to such a degree that one no longer saw it with the prejudiced eye of the native, referring everything to himself and to his own needs when he looks at it. We know how ill we see the things amongst which we live and that it is often necessary for someone to come from a distance to tell us what surrounds us. And so they had to remove things to a distance, that they might be able later to approach them with greater justice and calmly, with less familiarity, observing a reverend distance. For men only began to understand Nature when they no longer understood it; when they felt that it was the Other, indifferent towards men, without senses by which to apprehend us, then for the first time they stepped outside of Nature, alone, out of a lonely world.

And this was necessary, if man was to be an artist in dealing with it; the artist must not think of it any longer in its practical significance for man, but look at it objectively as a great, present reality.

It was thus that man was thought of in the period when he was painted great; but man had become hesitant and uncertain, and his image melted away in transformations, almost eluding any further portrayal. Nature was more permanent and greater, all movement in it was broader, and all repose simpler and more solitary. There was a longing in man to speak of himself with the sublime means which she offered, as of something equally real, and so we have the pictures of landscape in which nothing happens. Empty seas were painted, white houses on rainy days, roads on which no one is walking, and inexpressibly solitary water. Pathos was increasingly absent, and the better this language was understood, the more simply it was used. The artist immersed himself in the great quietness of things, he felt how their existence was passed within laws, without expectancy and without impatience. And the animals passed quietly amongst them and suffered, like them, the day and the night and were full of laws. And, later, when man appears in these surroundings, as shepherd, as peasant, or simply as a figure emerging from the depth of the picture, all presumption has fallen away from him, and one can see that he desires to be a thing.

In this growth of landscape-art into a slow transformation of the world into landscape, there is a long human development. The content of these pictures, resulting so unintentionally from observation and work, speaks to us of a future that has begun in our own time: tells us that man is no longer the social entity, moving with poise amongst his like, nor is he any longer one for whom evening and morning, for whom proximity and distance exist. It tells us, that he is placed amongst things like a thing, infinitely alone, and that all which is common to them both has withdrawn from things and men into the common depth, where the roots of all growth drink.

Worpswede

THE history of landscape-painting has not so far been written, and yet it is one of the works for which we have waited for years. The writer of it will have a big and unusual task, a task confusing by reason of its novelty and profundity. Anyone who undertook to record the history of portrait-painting or of the religious picture would have a long road to travel; thorough knowledge would have to be accessible to him, like a well-arranged reference-library. The sureness and integrity of his seeing would have to be as great as his visual memory; he would have to be able to see colours and to express colours, he would need to have command of the language of a poet and the presence of mind of an orator, if he were not to be embarrassed by the mass of material facing him, and the scales of his style would have to show with clearly visible deflexion even the finest shades of difference. He would need to be not only a historian, but also a psychologist who had learnt from life, a sage, who can reproduce in words Monna Lisa's smiling as well as the ageing expression of Titian's Charles V and the absent-minded, lost gaze of Jan Six in the Amsterdam collection. But, at any rate, he would be dealing with human beings, speaking of human beings and extolling man in getting to know him. He would be surrounded by the finest human faces, looked upon by the most beautiful, by the most earnest, by the most unforgettable eyes in the world; being surrounded by the smiles of famous lips and held fast by hands which have a curiously independent life of their own, he would have to keep constantly before him man as his chief concern, as the essential factor to which things and animals point in silent agreement, as if to the goal and perfecting of their inarticulate or unconscious life. But whoever was to write the history of landscape would find himself immediately, without aids, at the mercy of what was alien, unrelated, incomprehensible to him. We are accustomed to deal with forms, and landscape has no form, we are accustomed to deduce acts of volition from movements, and landscape, when it has movement, does not *will*. The waters flow, and in them the images of things fluctuate and tremble. And in the wind, which rustles in the ancient trees, the young forests grow up, grow into a future, which we shall not live to see. With human beings, we are in the habit of learning much from their hands and everything from their face, in which, as on a dial, the hours are visible which cradle and carry their soul. But landscape is without hands and has no face—or rather it is all face and has a terrible and dispiriting effect on man by reason of the great and incalculable quality of its features, somewhat in the manner of that "ghostly appearance" in the famous drawing of the Japanese painter Hokusai. For let it be confessed: landscape is foreign to us, and we are fearfully alone amongst trees which blossom and by streams which flow. Alone with the dead one is not nearly so defenceless as when alone with Trees. For, however mysterious death may be, life that is not our life is far more mysterious, life that is not concerned with us, and which, without seeing us, celebrates its festivals, as it were, at which we look on with a certain embarrassment, like chance guests who speak another language.

It is true, many people would cite our connexion with Nature, in whom we have our origin and in whom we are the final fruits of a great ascending genealogical tree. He who does that cannot, however, deny that, when we trace this genealogical tree downwards from ourselves, shoot by shoot, branch by branch, it is very soon lost in darkness; in a darkness inhabited by extinct mammoths, by monsters full of hatred and hostility, and that we come, the further back we go, to increasingly strange and horrible beings, so that we are forced to assume that, ultimately, we shall find Nature as the most horrible and strangest of all. The fact that we have had intercourse with Nature for thousands of years is of little significance here; for this intercourse has been very one-sided. It always seems that Nature does not know at all that we cultivate her and timidly put a small part of her forces to our own use. In many places we increase her fertility and in others we choke, with the pavement of our cities, wonderful springs ready to rise from the soil. We divert the rivers to our factories, but they are oblivious of the machines which they drive. We play with obscure forces, which we cannot lay hold of, by the names we give them, as children play with fire, and it seems for a moment as if all the energy had lain unused in things until we came to apply it to our transitory life and its needs. But repeatedly throughout the millenaries these forces shake off their names and rise like an oppressed class against their little lords, no, not even *against*—they simply rise, and civilizations fall from the shoulders of the earth, which becomes large and spacious once again and alone with its seas, its stars, and its trees.

It makes little difference that we change the uppermost surface of the earth, that we regulate its forests and meadows and get coal and metals from its crust, that we receive the fruits of the trees as though they were destined for us, when we remember at the same time one single hour in which Nature acted irrespective of us, our hopes, our life, with that sublime loftiness and indifference which fill all her movements. She knows nothing of us. And whatever men may have achieved, no man has been great enough to cause her to sympathize with his pain, to share in his rejoicing. Sometimes she has accompanied great and immortal hours of history with her mighty, tumultuous music, or has seemed, at a moment of decision, to stand silent, windless, holding her breath, or to surround a moment of harmless social gaiety with fluttering blossom, hovering butterflies, and dancing winds—but only at the next moment to turn aside and leave in the lurch those with whom she seemed just now to have shared everything.

The ordinary man, who lives with men, and sees Nature only in as far as she has reference to himself, is seldom aware of this problematic and uncanny relationship. He sees the surface of the things, which he and his like have created through the centuries, and likes to believe that the whole earth is concerned with him because a field can be cultivated, a forest thinned, and a river made navigable. His eye, focused almost entirely on men, sees Nature also, but incidentally, as something obvious and actual that must be exploited as much as possible. Children see Nature differently; solitary children in particular, who grow up amongst adults, foregather with her by a kind of like-mindedness and live within her, like the smaller animals, entirely at one with the happenings of forest and sky and in innocent, obvious harmony with them. But just because of this, there comes later for youth and maiden that lonely period filled with deep, trembling melancholy, when they feel unutterably forlorn, just at the time of their physical maturing; when they feel that the things and events in Nature have *no longer*, and their fellow-men have *not yet*, any sympathy for them. Spring comes, even when they are sad, the roses bloom, and the nights are full of nightingales, even though they would like to die; and when at last they would smile once more, the autumn days are there, the heavy days of November, which seem to fall without cessation, and on which a long sunless winter follows. And, on the other hand, they see people, equally strange to them and unconcerned, with their business, their cares, their successes and joys, and they do not understand it. And finally, some of them make up their minds and join these people in order to share their work and their fate, to be useful, to be helpful, to serve the enlargement of life somehow, whilst the others, unwilling to leave the Nature they have lost, go in pursuit of her and try now, consciously and by the use of their concentrated will, to come as near to her again as they were in their childhood without knowing it. It will be understood that the latter are artists: poets or painters, composers or architects, fundamentally lonely spirits, who, in turning to Nature, put the eternal above the transitory, that which is most profoundly based on law above that which is fundamentally ephemeral, and who, since they cannot persuade Nature to concern herself with them, see their task to be the understanding of Nature, so that they may take their place somewhere in her great design. And the whole of humanity comes nearer to Nature in these isolated and lonely ones. It is not the least and is, perhaps, the peculiar value of art, that it is the medium in which man and landscape, form and world, meet and find one another. In actuality they live beside one another, scarcely knowing aught of one another, and in the picture, the piece of architecture, the symphony, in a word, in art, they seem to come together in a higher, prophetic truth, to rely upon one another, and it is as if, by completing one another, they became that perfect unity, which is the very essence of a work of art.

From this point of view the theme and purpose of all art would seem to lie in the reconciliation of the Individual and the All, and the moment of exaltation, the artistically important Moment, would seem to be that in which the two scales of the balance counterpoise one another. And, indeed, it would be very tempting to show this relationship in various works of art; to show how a symphony mingles the voices of a stormy day with the tumult of our blood, how a building owes its character half to us and half to the forest. To make a portrait, is this not to see a human being like a landscape, and is there any landscape devoid of figures, which is not filled with what it has to tell us about the painter who has seen it? Strange relationships arise here. Often the two are placed side by side in rich, fruitful contrast, often the man appears to derive from the landscape, at another time the landscape from the man, and then again their relationship is that of equals and brothers. Nature seems to draw near to man for some moments, when she lends even to cities the appearance of landscape, and humanity, with its centaurs, mermaids, and old men of the sea, with Böcklin's blood in their veins, draws near to Nature. But it is always a question of this relationship, not least in poetry, which is able to say most about the soul precisely when it presents landscape, and which, if it found man in that limitless and empty space, in which it has pleased Goya to place him, could only despair of expressing the deepest truth about him.

Art knew man before it concerned itself with landscape. Man stood in front of the landscape and hid it, the Madonna stood in front of it, the lovely, gentle Italian woman with the playful child, and far behind her the heavens sounded and a countryside echoed tones which were like the opening words of an Ave Maria. This landscape, spread out in the background of Umbrian and Tuscan pictures, is like a soft accompaniment played with one hand, not inspired by reality but copied from the trees, roads, and clouds which affectionate memory has retained. Man was the chief concern, the real theme of art, and, as lovely women are adorned with precious stones, so he was adorned with fragments of that Nature which the artist was not yet capable of viewing as a whole.

They must have been different, these artists who looked past their fellow-men to see the landscape, great, indifferent, mighty Nature. Men like Jacob Ruysdael, solitary figures, who lived like children amongst grown-ups and died poor and forgotten. Man lost his importance, he withdrew before the great, simple, inexorable things, which towered above him and outlived him. The artist must not, for this reason, desist from painting him, on the contrary, he had learnt, by his conscientious and thorough treatment of Nature, to see man better and with juster perception. Man had become smaller, was no longer the centre of the world; he had become greater, for the artist looked at him with the eyes with which he looked at Nature; he was of no more importance than a tree, but he was of great importance, because the tree is of great importance.

Is this not, perhaps, the secret and sublimity of Rembrandt, that he saw and painted people as landscape? By the means of the light and the twilight, by which the very spirit of morning or the mystery of evening is realized, he told of the life of those whom he painted, creating spaciousness and power. It is indeed surprising to see how greatly he dispenses with trees, in his Biblical pictures and drawings, in order to use people as trees and bushes. Think of the "Hundred Florin Plate": does not the crowd of beggars and of sick folk crawl along by the walls like low, multi-branched undergrowth, and does not the figure of Christ stand on the edge of the ruin like a towering solitary tree? We do not know many landscapes by Rembrandt, and yet he was a landscape-painter, the greatest there has ever been, perhaps, and one of the very greatest painters. He was able to paint portraits, because he looked deep into faces as into countries with a wide horizon and a lofty, cloudy sky, filled with movement. In the few portraits that Böcklin painted (I am thinking particularly of the self-portraits), a similar conception of the subject as landscape is to be noted, and if portraiture interested him so little otherwise, was even actually distasteful to him, it is because he could see only a few people in this landscape manner. For him, who had been spoiled by the immense richness of Nature, man was a limitation, an individual case, which disturbed and interrupted the broad, exuberant, emotional life in which he lived. When he needed him, he put a figure in his place. Creatures which seem born of the trees traverse his pictures, and the sea that he paints is filled with noisy, laughing life. All the elements seem to be fertile and to people a world, in which man cannot appear, with their sons and daughters. Böcklin who strove, as scarcely any other has done, to lay hold of Nature, saw the gulf that separates her from man, and he paints her as a mystery, the way Leonardo painted woman, self-contained, indifferent, with a smile that eludes us so soon as we attempt to refer it to ourselves.

Into the landscapes of Anselm Feuerbach and of Puvis de Chavannes also (to mention but two masters) only silent, timeless figures entered, emerging from the depths of their pictures and living, as it were, on the far side of a mirror. And this shyness towards man runs through all landscape-painting. One of the greatest masters, Théodore Rousseau, dispensed with any figure whatsoever, and nowhere in his work do we miss it. So unnecessary is man for his almost mathematically correct world. Others tended to give life to their roads and meadows with animals walking or grazing; with cows, whose broad-sided lethargy stood massive and peaceful on the surface of the picture; with sheep, carrying through the twilight the light of the evening sky on their woolly backs; with birds, enveloped in the vibrating air, as they settled in the high tree-tops. And then with the flocks there came into the pictures, unintentionally, the shepherd, the first human being in the tremendous solitude. In Millet, he stands as quiet as a tree, the one upright thing in the wide plain of Barbizon. He does not move; he stands like a blind man amongst his sheep, like a thing thoroughly familiar to them, and his dress is heavy as earth and weathered like stone. He has no particular life of his own. His life is that of this plain and of this sky and of these animals surrounding him. He has no memory, for his impressions are rain and wind and noon and sunset, and he has no need to retain them because they always come again. And all these figures of Millet are similar, their silhouette standing so quiet and tree-like against the sky, or, as if bent by an incessant wind, appearing in relief against the dark soil. Millet once wrote to Thoré: "I want the people I depict to look as if they were part of their situation, and it to be impossible to think that the idea of being anything else could occur to them." But the situation in which they find themselves is work. Quite definite, daily work, work on this land, that has formed them, as the wind by the sea forms the sparse trees which stand on the edge of the dunes. This work, by which they receive their food, attaches them firmly, as by a strong root, to this ground to which they belong, like sturdy plants that wrest a bare existence from stony land.

Just as language has no longer anything in common with the things it names, so the movements of most of the people who live in cities have lost their connexion with the earth; they hang, as it were, in the air, hover in all directions, and find no place where they can settle. The peasants painted by Millet still have the few large movements which are quiet and simple and move towards the earth by the most direct way. And man, the exacting, nervous inhabitant of cities, feels himself ennobled in these stolid peasants. He, who is not in harmony with anything, sees in them beings who pass their lives nearer to Nature, indeed, he tends to see in them heroes, because of this, although Nature remains as hard and indifferent towards them as she is towards him. And perhaps it may seem to him for a while as if man had built cities only that he might not see Nature and her sublime indifference (which we call beauty), and to console himself with the seeming nature of the sea of houses, which is man-made and continually repeats itself and man, as if by means of large mirrors. Millet hated Paris. And if he made a practice of going out of the village in the opposite direction to that of his friend Rousseau, this was, perhaps, because the enclosed effect of the forest reminded him too much of the narrowness of the town, because the tall trees could easily suggest high walls, like the walls from which he had fled, as from a prison. The elements of his art, which might be called, as far as the figures are concerned, solitude and gesture, are not really figure-values but the corresponding values of landscape. The plain corresponds to the solitude, the sky to the movement, which is seen against it. He, also, is a landscape-painter. His figures are great by reason of what is about them and the line which separates them from their surroundings. The earth and the sky are his subject. Millet introduced both of these into painting, but he is frequently able to give only the contour instead of the light streaming out of the sky on all sides. His contour was large, sure, monumental, it is the eternal factor in his work, but it often points to the draughtsman or the plastic artist rather than to the painter.

Here we must mention the lowing cow by Segantini in the famous picture in the Berlin National Gallery. The line by which the animal's back is drawn against the sky, this unforgettable line, has the strength and clarity of Millet, but it is not motionless, it trembles and vibrates like a sounding string, touched by the pure light of this lofty world of mountain solitude.

This painter is more closely related to Millet than we think. He is not a painter of the mountains. The hills are for him only ascents to new plains, over which rises a sky that is large like Millet's sky, but deeper and filled with more light and colour. He sought this sky all his life long and when he had found it, he died. He died close on 3,000 metres up, beyond human habitation, and Nature stood in silent, blind grandeur about his hard death. She knew nothing of him either. But when he painted the mother with the child into the immeasurable radiance of that untouched world, he was as close to human life as he was to that other life, the sublime life of Nature, by which he was surrounded.

There was a great love of Nature in the German Romantics. But they loved her as the hero of a story by Turgeniev loved his sweetheart, of whom he said: "I am particularly fond of Sophia when I sit with my back to her, that's to say, when I think of her, when I see her before me with my mind's eye, especially in the evening, on the terrace . . ." Only one of them, perhaps, has looked Nature in the face: Philipp Otto Runge, the Hamburg artist, who painted the Nightingale Bush and the Morning. The great miracle of the sunrise has not been painted like that again. The increasing light, rising silent and radiant to the stars, and on the earth beneath the cabbage-field, still completely saturated with the strong, dewy depth of night, in which a little naked child—Morning—is lying. Everything here has been seen and seen again. We feel the cool of many mornings, when the painter rose before the sun and went out, trembling with expectation, to look upon each scene of the mighty spectacle and to miss nothing of the exciting action beginning there. This picture was painted with a beating heart. It is a landmark. It opens up not one but a thousand new ways of approach to Nature. Runge felt this himself. In his *Literary Remains*, which appeared in 1842, the following passage occurs: "The whole tendency is towards landscape, seeking something definite in this indefiniteness. Yet our artists are reverting to history and losing their way. Is there not then in this new art—the trivial art of landscape, if you like—a supreme objective to be achieved? which will, perhaps, be still more beautiful than previous achievements?"

Philipp Otto Runge wrote those words at the beginning of the nineteenth century, but much later the "trivial art of landscape" was still regarded as an almost subordinate occupation, and in our Academies it was commonly held that landscape-painters were not in the full sense painters. These institutions had every reason to fear the competition of Nature, to which Dürer had already drawn attention with such reverent simplicity.

A stream of young people poured out of the dusty rooms of the Academies, they sought out the villages, they began to see, they painted peasants and trees and exalted the masters of Fontainebleau, who had attempted all this half a century earlier. It was, at any rate, an honest urge which lay behind this movement, but it was only a movement, and it may well have carried along with it many for whom the Academy was not in any real sense too narrow. It was necessary to wait. Of all who went forth thus, many returned later to the cities, not without having learnt something, indeed, perhaps not without having become fundamentally changed. Others wandered from landscape to landscape, everywhere learning; discriminatingly eclectic, for whom the world became a school—some became famous, many disappeared, and new artists are growing up, who will judge them.

But not far from the district in which Philipp Otto Runge painted his Morning, beneath the same sky, so to say, there is a remarkable landscape, where a small group of young people had settled at that time, dissatisfied with the school, longing to find themselves, and determined to take their life in hand somehow. They have not left that place, indeed they have even avoided making journeys of any distance, being always afraid of missing something, some irreplaceable sunset, some grey autumn day, or the hour when the first spring flowers issue from the earth after nights of storm. The important things of the world fell away from them, and they experienced that great revaluation of all values, which Constable had experienced before them, writing in a letter: "The world is wide, no two days are alike, not even two hours; since the creation of the world there have been no two leaves of a tree identical." A man who has arrived at this knowledge begins a new life. Nothing is behind him, everything is before him and "The world is wide."

These young people, who had sat in the Academies for years, impatient and dissatisfied, felt the urge—as Runge wrote—"for landscape, they sought something definite in this indefiniteness". Landscape is definite, it is devoid of chance, and every falling leaf fulfils, as it falls, one of the greatest laws of the universe. It is this adherence to law, which never hesitates and fulfils itself at every moment calmly and peacefully, that makes nature such an experience for young people. It is just this that they are seeking, and when, in their perplexity, they desire a master, they are not thinking of someone who will continually interfere with their development and disturb, with a rough hand, the mysterious hours in which the crystallization of their souls takes place; they want an example. They want to see a life, beside them, over them, about them, a life that lives without concerning itself with them. The great figures of history live in this manner, but they are not visible, and one must close one's eyes in order to see them. But young people do not willingly close their eyes, especially when they are painters: they turn to Nature and, in seeking it, they seek themselves.

It is interesting to see how a different aspect of Nature acts educatively and challengingly on each generation; this generation fought its way through to clarity by wandering in forests, that one needed hills and castles in order to find itself. Our soul is other than that of our fathers; we can still understand the castles and ravines, the sight of which caused them to grow, but we make no progress by such means. Our feeling is increased by no shade, our thoughts are not multiplied a thousandfold, we feel as if we were in somewhat old-fashioned rooms, where the imagination can see no future. The thing we need is what our fathers drove past in closed coaches, with impatience, and plagued by boredom. Where they opened their mouths to yawn, we open our eyes to gaze; for we live under the sign of the plain and the sky. These are two words, but they express really a single experience: the plain. The plain is the feeling by which we grow. We understand it and it provides a kind of model for us; everything in it is significant for us: the great circle of the horizon and the few things standing simply and solemnly against the sky. And this sky, of whose changing darkness and light every one of the thousand leaves on a bush seems to speak in different words, and which, when night comes, contains far more stars than those dense and unspacious skies above cities, forests and mountains. It is in such a plain that the painters live, about whom I shall have to speak. To it they owe what they have become and much more besides: to its greatness and inexhaustibility they owe their continuing development.

It is a strange land. If you stand on the little sandhill of Worpswede, you can see it spread out all round, like the peasants' kerchiefs with their dark centre and their corners showing flowers of a deep brilliance. It lies flat before you, with scarcely a fold, and the roads and water-courses lead far into the horizon. A sky begins there of indescribable variety and spaciousness. It is reflected in every leaf. Everything seems to be occupied with it; it is everywhere.

And the sea is everywhere. The sea, that is no longer, that ebbed and flowed here thousands of years ago, whose dune was the sandhill on which Worpswede lies. These things cannot forget it. The great murmuring filling the old pines on the hill seems to be its murmur, and the wind, the mighty, sweeping wind, brings the smell of it. The sea is the story of this land. It has hardly any other past.

Once, when the sea withdrew, it began to take shape. Plants unknown to us appeared and there was quick and hasty growth in the rich layers of mud. But the sea always returned, with its highest tides, to the regions it had left, as if it could not be separated from them, and in the end there remained black, boggy marshes full of watery creatures and slowly decaying fertility. The flats lay thus solitary, completely self-engrossed, for centuries. The heath was formed. And finally it began, at isolated spots, to close up as a wound closes. About this time, which is generally reckoned to be the thirteenth century, monasteries were founded in the Weser valley, which sent Dutch colonists into these districts, into a hard, uncertain life. Later there followed (at rare enough intervals) fresh attempts at colonization in the sixteenth century, in the seventeenth, but only in the eighteenth was there a definite plan, the energetic carrying out of which rendered the lands by the Weser, by the Hamme, Wümme and Wörpe, permanently inhabitable. To-day they are fairly well populated. The early settlers, as far as they were able to persist, grew rich by the sale of the turf, their successors led a life of labour and poverty, close to the earth, as if under the compulsion of a stronger force of gravity. Something of the sadness and homelessness of their fathers lies upon them, their fathers, who left a life behind them when they went forth into the black, boggy land to begin a new life, knowing not how it would end. There is no family likeness amongst these people; the mothers' way of smiling is not passed on to the sons, because their mothers have never smiled. They all have but the *one* face: the hard, tense face of work, the skin of which has been stretched by all their labours so that in old age it is too large, as a much-worn glove is too large. One sees arms made disproportionately long by the lifting of heavy objects, and backs of women and old men grown crooked, like trees which have stood always in the same storm. The heart in these bodies is crushed and has not unfolded. The mind is freer and has developed in a certain one-sided way. No increase of depth, but a sharpening of it in inventiveness, maliciousness, quick-wittedness. Their language helps them there. This Low German (Platt) has a natural vitality in it, with its short, taut, colourful words, that move as if with atrophied wings and webbed feet like marshland birds. It is to the point, and passes over easily into noisy, clattering laughter, it learns from the occasion, it imitates sounds, but is not enriched from within outwards: it makes a beginning. It is heard often far off during the midday rest, when the heavy labour of turf-cutting, compelling silence, is interrupted. It is rarely heard in the evening, when weariness comes early and sleep enters the houses almost with twilight.

These houses stand widely scattered on the long straight "damms"; they are red, with green or blue timbering, smothered by thick, heavy straw roofs, and seem to be pressed down into the earth by their massive, pelt-like burden. Many of them can scarcely be seen from the damms; they have drawn the trees across their faces as protection from the never-ceasing winds. Their windows flash through the thick foliage, like jealous eyes looking out from a dark mask. They stand there peacefully, the smoke from the hearth filling them completely and flowing out of the black depth of the door and oozing through the cracks in the roof. On cool days it hangs round about the house, repeating its shape in sizes as large again and ghostly-grey. Within, the whole is practically one room, a wide, long-shaped room, in which the smell and the warmth of the cattle unite with the acrid fumes of the open fire to make a strange twilight, in which it would be quite possible to lose one's bearings. This "Diele" widens out further back, there are windows on the right and on the left, and straight ahead are the bedrooms. They contain little furniture. A spacious table, several chairs, a corner-cupboard with some glass and ware, and the enclosed, large bed-compartments with sliding doors. In this bed-cupboard the children are born, the hours of death and the wedding nights are passed. There, into this last, narrow, windowless darkness life has withdrawn, ousted from every other place in the whole house by work.

Into this existence the festivals fall with a strange directness, the weddings, the baptisms, the funerals. With a stiff awkwardness the peasants range themselves about the coffin, with a stiff awkwardness they shuffle through the wedding-dance. They spend their sadness on their work, and their pleasure is a reaction from the earnestness which work imposes on them. There are "characters" amongst them, wags and wisecrackers, cynics and ghost-seers. Some can tell of America, others have never been further than Bremen. Some live in a certain contentment and peace, read the Bible and believe in order; many are unhappy, have lost children, and their wives, worn out by want and labour, die by slow degrees; perhaps here and there one of them grows up filled with a vague, deep, clamant longing—perhaps—but work is stronger than any of them.

In spring, when the turf-making begins, they rise with the first light and spend the entire day in the turf-pit, dripping with moisture, made one with the moor by the disguise of their black, muddy clothing as they shovel the moor-earth, heavy as lead, up out of it. In summer the cut turf dries whilst they are busy with the hay and corn harvests, and in the autumn they take it in boats and carts into the town. They travel for hours.

The shrill alarm-clock often wakens them at midnight. The loaded boat is waiting for them on the black water of the canal, and then they travel solemnly, as if with coffins, towards the dawn and the town, both of which are slow to appear.

And what are the painters doing amongst these people? To that we must reply, that they do not live amongst them, but, as it were, facing them, as they stand facing the trees and all the things which grow and move in the flood of the damp, resonant air. They come from distant parts. They force these people, who are not of their kind, into the landscape; and this is no act of violence. The strength of a child suffices for it—and Runge wrote: "We must become children, if we want to achieve the best." They want to achieve the best, and they have become children. They see everything in one breath, people and things. Just as the peculiar, colour-filled light of this high sky does not differentiate but embodies everything that rises up in it and rests in it with the same kindness, so they exercise a certain naïve justice when, without reflection, they feel people and things, which stand quietly side by side, to be phenomena of the same atmosphere, manifesting colours rendered luminous by it to life. In this they do no one an injustice. They do not help these people, they do not teach them, they do not improve them. They bring nothing into their life, which remains what it always was, a life in misery and darkness, but they bring forth out of the depth of this life a truth, which causes them to grow themselves, or, not to exaggerate, a probability, that one can love. Maeterlinck, in his wonderful book on bees, says in one place: "There is not yet any truth, but everywhere there are three good probabilities. Each man chooses one for himself, or better, it chooses him, and this choice, which he makes or which is made of him, often happens quite by instinct. He holds by it henceforth, and it determines the form and content of everything that enters into his consciousness." And then the three probabilities are illustrated by an example, by a group of peasants putting up stooks of corn on the edge of a plain. There is the short-sighted probability of the romantic, beautifying all he looks at; the relentless, cruel probability of the realist; and, finally, the quiet, deep probability of the wise man, which is trustful towards unexplored complexities, a probability which, perhaps, comes nearest to the truth. Not far from this probability lies the naïve probability of the artist. By putting men with things, he raises them: for he is the friend, the confidant, the poet of things. But men do not become better or worse thereby, to quote Maeterlinck's words again: "Progress is not necessary to cause the spectacle to fill us with enthusiasm. The enigma suffices . . ." And in this sense the artist seems to stand above the wise man. Where the latter endeavours to solve enigmas, the artist has a far greater task, or, if you will, a still greater right. The artist's function is—to love the enigma. All art is this: love, which has been poured out over enigmas—and all works of art are enigmas surrounded, adorned, enveloped by love.

And there lay before these young people, who had come in order to find themselves, the many enigmas of this country. The birch-trees, the moorland cottages, the stretches of heath, the people, the evenings and the days, of which no two are alike, and in which no two hours could be interchanged one with another.

These are the people about whom I shall write in what follows, not in the form of criticism nor with the pretension of saying anything conclusive. That would hardly be possible; since they are people who are still developing, who change, who grow, who, perhaps at the moment of the writing of these words, are creating something which will contradict all that has gone before. It may be that I have written only of what is past; that also has its value. What I here give an account of is ten years of work, ten years of serious, lonely German work. And, in addition, the qualifying limitation, which must always be assumed where an attempt is made to trace a man's life interpretatively, holds good here as elsewhere: "We shall often have to call a halt before the unknown."

From the Dream-Book

(The seventh, eleventh and twenty-sixth dream)

THE SEVENTH DREAM

I LOOKED for the girl. I found her in a long, narrow room, in which the morning-light was just breaking. She was sitting on a chair and was smiling almost imperceptibly. Beside her, not more than a pace distant, was another chair, on which a young man was sitting, leaning back stiffly. It seemed as if the two had passed the night in this way.

The girl moved and held out her hand to me, raising it high to do so. The hand felt warm and somehow rough, as if one were holding a little animal that lived in the open and had to fend for itself.

And now the young man moved too. He was obviously making an effort to wake up; his face grimaced in an unpleasing and impatient manner. The girl had turned a little sideways and was watching him. His face was quite red with the effort; it contracted towards the centre and now and then one eyelid lifted with a twitch. But the eye beneath it seemed empty.

"That's no good," said the girl, her transparent voice scintillating with dissolved laughter, "you can't wake up, if your eyes are not back again."

I was about to ask, what did she mean by that? But all at once I understood. Of course. I recalled a young Russian worker from the country who still held the belief, when he came to Moscow, that the stars were the eyes of God and the eyes of the angels. They talked him out of it. They could not contradict it at all, but they could talk him out of it. And rightly so. For the stars are the eyes of human beings, which rise out of their closed lids and become bright and regain their strength. And that is why all the stars are above the country-side, where everyone is sleeping, and over the town there are only a few, because there are so many restless people there, weeping and reading, laughing and watching, who keep their eyes.

This girl ought to have told the Russian that. But she had been thinking of other things for some time. She was telling about someone, about a girl, as I understood it, who was now married in Meran. Now she's called ——, and she mentioned a name, with much amusement. I nodded, nodded perhaps too much. "Now, of course, you know something," she said mockingly. "The way you always ask names and want to know names and behave as if that meant something." "My dear," I said seriously, "that does mean something amongst men. Roses are called Marie Baumann or Madame Testout or the Countess of Camondo or Emotion, but that's almost superfluous. They don't know their names. We hang a little wooden label on them, and they don't remove it. That is all. But human beings know their names; they are interested in what they are called, they learn them by heart and tell them to anyone who asks. They nourish them, so to say, all their lives, and in the end grow very like them, indistinguishable from them, except in some small detail——"

But I was talking uselessly. The girl was not listening. She had risen, was standing at the window, where it was already day, smiling and calling someone. A bird, I think.

THE ELEVENTH DREAM

Then there was a street. We were going down it together, keeping step, close to each other. Her arm was lying across my shoulders.

The street was wide, with the emptiness of morning, a Boulevard, slightly downhill, sloping just so much as would be needed to take the little bit of weight from a child's step. She walked as if little wings were on her feet.

I was thinking of——

"What were you thinking of——?" she asked after a time.

"I was thinking——" I said slowly, without looking at the girl, "I was thinking of a street far away in an eastern town, which was as broad, as empty, as bright, only it was much, much steeper. I was sitting in a little carriage. The horse in front of it had taken charge of the situation. I was in no further doubt: it was beginning to bolt. The coachman acted accordingly. From behind he looked as if he had no head, and his massive back was being tugged at, like a knot that someone tries to undo in a temper, making it all the time tighter.

"The little carriage tore along, as if it were tearing the road with it and the houses and everything, and as if nothing behind it remained standing. And below, at the end of the street, was the river, a splendid, self-conscious, famous river, and it was shining. I saw how bright it was. Then I saw the sky full of the morning and of lofty, lively winds. Then I saw the coachman's back again, that hid everything. I imagined that he was shouting, but it was impossible to know that because of the noise of the carriage. Again I saw the sky, which promised a really fine day; and suddenly I caught sight of the horse for a moment, a ghostly animal, far too large for us, and I felt almost convinced that it did not belong to us at all. I saw, as if I had the time, a child in a doorway, playing quietly. I saw a tavern at a street-corner; beside the door a bottle was painted on a metal sign, a small, crooked, thick, queer bottle; it was highly questionable whether such a bottle existed anywhere. A window opening somewhere blinded me; then, for the fraction of a second, I saw a horrible face and then———"

"But that was as far as I remembered."

"I know why you remembered . . ." said the girl.

"Yes, because we are walking. And because I felt very much the same then, in those strangely detailed moments, in which I saw a lot, as I do now. As if it were the same thing at bottom; the same feeling, the same wave of feelings, things, thoughts, brilliance and movement that carried everything along with it———"

"You are extraordinary," said the girl, whilst we continued to go down the broad, bright street. "You think, you do hardly anything else, and yet everything escapes you. Did you really not know till now that joy is something terrible of which one is not afraid? One goes right through a terror to its very end: and that is just joy. A terror, of which one does not know even the first letter. A terror that one trusts.—Or were you afraid?"

"I don't know," I said in confusion. "I cannot answer you."

THE TWENTY-SIXTH DREAM

"Taken away from here and placed under a glass dome," said the girl, facing into the adjacent room. Then she came right in and shut the door, drawing it quietly towards her.

"Claire," I said, impelled by the feeling that everything had been exactly like this once before; Claire was what one had had to say at this point before. But this time, things went differently, so differently that it would have been permissible to say anything: cobalt or breathlessness or carp, but not that, not that: Claire. It was a mistake, it was offensive, it was frankly impossible to say Claire at that moment.

I saw that at once and understood it so perfectly, that the contempt with which the girl turned away from me did not surprise me at all. I heard her opening a drawer somewhere, and a little after that she was standing at the window with a piece of sewing, held it up against the light, stretched it out, and looked at it with her head slightly on one side. And in this position she said disdainfully: "It is incomprehensible, that you did not want to kiss her."

Now that was a quite unjustifiable sarcasm, and I contented myself with a slight ironical gesture. The girl sat down on the broad window-seat, laid her piece of sewing over one knee, and smoothed it out slowly to the right and to the left with both hands. And under the influence of this smoothing movement, or because I was looking at the fair drooping hair of the girl, or heaven knows for what reason, I actually see that it is incomprehensible. An enormous incomprehensibility comes towards me out of a small recollection. I see eyes, the enlarged eyes of a consumptive, and these eyes implored. Good heavens, how these eyes implored.

"There will not be much left of her by now," said the girl.

FROM THE DREAM-BOOK

Her two hands lay on the work on her knee, and it seemed, as she leant back and looked at me, that she put as much distance as possible between herself and them.

She looked at me, but she made her look so distant that I lost, as it were, all my contours in it.

"She was a servant-girl," I said quickly, as if in answer to a question, and as if it were the last moment for such an explanation. And I was unconscious that I then continued to say:

"She was (I must have said) in the large hotel, inhabited mostly by invalids. I stayed there, however, scarcely a week. She served me. I noticed that she served me well; by the third day, she knew everything, knew my little habits and petted them. But she coughed. She had caught the infection. 'You have a cough,' I said one morning. She only smiled. Immediately afterwards, outside, she had another attack.

"Then I left. When I opened my trunk in Florence, one tray was entirely covered with violets. And that evening a little note fluttered out of my night things. Farewell was written on it. Like a dictation written in school.

"Naturally I did not think of her again. Yes, I did; two months later when I visited the hotel again, which invalids generally inhabit, and she was not there, I even asked for her. 'Marie is ill,' the new chambermaid said, as if offended. But in the evening she was there. It was April and the climate of the place was famous. But that evening it was remarkably cold. She was kneeling before my stove, and when her face turned towards me it came out of the glow of the fire. Her eyes were shining from the fire. She did not get up at once, and I noticed that she had difficulty in rising. I helped her a little. I felt how light she was. 'Are you all right?' I said carelessly and as if intending a pleasantry. I remember she made no response; she simply looked at me, looked at me, looked at me. Not close to me; she had stepped back to the cupboard. I think she found it difficult to stand. The twilight in the room had no consideration for us. It was growing dark. There was nothing to ease the situation. The heavy weight of it was on her alone. For I was simply embarrassed and restless, even impatient. In the end, however, she had got the better of it, and came (she had some strength still, still some strength), came and looked at me once again quite close. How dark it was. It seemed to me as if her hair had grown softer, from her illness perhaps, or because she had not been working latterly. She raised her arms slightly (I nearly forgot that) and laid both hands flat on my breast. That was the last thing before she went——"

At that point I stopped, taken aback. "Have I been talking all this time?" I asked disconcertedly in the direction of the girl. At first I did not see her at all; she was sitting in a big green-covered easy chair, which had not been by the window before. She was sitting bent over her work, just a little more, possibly, than was necessary.

"And you?" she said suddenly. She did not even look up.

"I, yes, . . . I let her go. I did nothing. I said nothing either. I looked for something which was of no importance and insignificant."

The girl looked up critically, with that disturbing darkness in her glance which comes into some blue eyes when they have been looking down for a while.

"And then?" she asked.

"Then I turned on the light."

She was busy again. She turned her work to the right and to the left, then held it away and looked at it as far off as possible, with head thrown back and half-closed eyes.

"I went to bed pretty soon," I recalled, "I was tired. Or no, I read a bit; yes, I read——"

And I hoped to remember in the silence, what it could have been that I had read then.

But with quick decision and, as it seemed to me, without much care she laid her work on the window-seat and collected the coloured threads which remained in her lap.

"Read," she said suddenly with scorn, looking up quickly with completely cold impenetrable eyes. "Read——" she repeated with indescribable hardness.

The word, as she said it, lost its meaning. I felt as if she had spoken the name of an illness, which was prevalent, an infectious illness, of which many people were dying. I shuddered, as if it had just attacked me.

The girl had now clasped her hands round one of her knees which she had raised; her face was turned away towards the window, and, speaking in that direction, she said: "Good God ——" with the emphasis on the first, long syllable.

At last I could stand it no longer. I advanced a few steps towards the window. I felt words rising up within me, which I must say only to——

At that point voices sounded in the next room. It was as if a whole bundle of confused voices was being thrown against the door, and a second time—and we were both standing there, it seemed to me, seized by the same fear.

An Encounter

Any road outside the town. (The only condition, that no one else is on it.) The dog is suddenly there, like a sudden idea. He behaves deliberately in a doggish way, apparently entirely preoccupied with his own trivial affairs, from which he sends, unnoticed, remarkably definite glances aimed at the stranger, who continues on his way. Not one of these glances is lost. The dog is now in front of, now beside the wayfarer, all the time observing him furtively with increasing excitement. Suddenly, catching up with the stranger:

Now then! Now then!

He emits exuberant signs of joy, trying, finally, in this way to stop the man who walks on. The latter makes a quick, friendly gesture, both calming and negative, and passes the dog easily by stepping half a pace to the left.

The dog in joyful expectancy:

It is still to come.

He gulps from excess of emotion. Finally, with upward-reaching face, he flings himself in front of the man again, who is striding rapidly forward: Now it is coming, he thinks, and holds his face forward, urgently, to show he understands. Now it is coming.

What? says the stranger, hesitating for a moment.

The expectation in the eyes of the dog changes to embarrassment, doubt, dismay. Well, if the man does not know, what ought to come, how then is it to come?—They must both know; only then can it come.

The stranger again takes half a step to the left, this time quite mechanically; he looks absent-minded. The dog keeps in front of him, trying—with scarcely any attempt now at caution—to look into the eyes of the stranger. At one moment he thinks their eyes have met, but their glances do not cleave to one another.

Is it possible that this small thing—thinks the dog.

AN ENCOUNTER

It is *not* a small thing, says the stranger suddenly, attentive and impatient.

The dog is taken aback: How (he controls himself with difficulty) if I feel, nevertheless, that we ... My instinct? ... my ...

Don't say it, exclaims the stranger, interrupting him almost angrily. They are standing opposite one another. This time their glances interpenetrate, the man's entering the dog's, as the knife its sheath.

The dog is the first to give way; he ducks, jumps to the side, and with a glance upward from below, which comes sideways from the right, confesses:

I want to do something for you. I would do anything for you. Anything.

The man is already walking on. He behaves as if he had not understood. He is walking apparently without paying attention, but now and then he tries to watch the dog. He sees him running about awkwardly and strangely at a loss, now ahead, now behind. All at once he is some paces in front, turned towards the man following him, in the attitude of scraping, stretched forward from his raised, taut hindquarters. With great self-conquest he makes some foolish and childishly playful movements, as if to create the illusion that he has something alive in his front paws. And then, without a word, he takes the stone, which fills this rôle, in his mouth.

Now I am innocuous and cannot say anything more; this is expressed in the nod of the head with which he looks back. There is something almost confidential in this nod, a kind of agreement, which must, however, for heaven's sake, not be taken too seriously. The whole thing is so by the way and just fun, and the carrying of the stone is taken that way too.

But now that the dog has the stone in his mouth, the man cannot help speaking:

Let us be sensible, he says as he walks on, without bending down to the dog.

It does not do us any good. What is the use of our making ourselves known to each other? There are some memories that must not be allowed to occur. I felt the same way for a while, and I nearly asked you who you were. You would have said I, for we don't use names between us. But, you see, that would not have helped. It would only have added to our confusion. For I can confess to you now, that for a while I was thoroughly disconcerted. Now I am calmer. If I could only convince you how much I feel the same about it. There are, if possible, more obstructions in my nature to prevent our meeting again. You would not believe how difficult things are for us.

When the stranger spoke like that, the dog had understood that there was no use in continuing the pretence of perfunctory play. For his part, he was glad of this, but at the same time he seemed filled with an increasing fear that he was going to interrupt the speaker.

Only now, when the stranger sees, with surprise and alarm, an animal before him in a hostile attitude, as he at first supposes, does the dog succeed in doing this. It is true that the stranger, in the next moment, knows that the dog, far from showing hate or enmity, is worried and anxious; this is clearly expressed by the timid brightness of his look and the way he holds his head on one side, and it is seen again in the way he is carrying the stone, lying hard and heavy between lips drawn back convulsively.

All at once the man understands, and he cannot withhold a passing smile:

You are right, my good fellow, it shall remain unspoken between us, the word that occasioned so many misunderstandings.

And the dog lays the stone down carefully, like something breakable, and at the side in order not to impede the stranger any longer.

The latter, in fact, goes on and, sunk in thought, does not notice until later that the dog is accompanying him unobtrusively, devotedly, without a mind of his own, the way a dog follows his master. He feels almost pained by it.

No, he says, no; not that way. Not after this experience. We should both forget what we have experienced to-day. The daily habit is blunting, and your nature tends to subordinate itself to mine. In the end a responsibility would grow up, which I cannot undertake. You would not notice at all how your whole confidence was placed in me; you would think too highly of me and expect from me what I cannot perform. You would watch me and would approve even of what is not good. If I want to give you a pleasure, shall I find it? And if you are sad one day and complaining—shall I be able to help you? And you are not to think that it is I who allow you to die. No, no, no. Go away, I beg of you: go away.

And the man almost began to run, and it looked as if he were fleeing from something. Only gradually did his pace slacken, and finally he was walking more slowly than before.

Slowly he thought: What else would have been said between us to-day? And how, in the end, we should have shaken hands.

An indescribable longing stirs in him. He stops and turns backward. But the bit of road immediately behind him turns into the twilight, which has fallen in the meantime, and there is no one to be seen.

An Experience

IT might be little more than a year ago, that something strange happened to him in the castle garden which sloped down fairly steeply to the sea. Walking up and down with a book, as was his wont, it occurred to him to lean against the forking of two branches, at about the level of his shoulder in a shrub-like tree, and immediately he felt himself so pleasantly supported in this attitude and given such ample rest, that he remained like this, without reading, completely absorbed into Nature, in a state of almost unconscious contemplation. Gradually his attention was awakened by a hitherto unknown sensation: it was as if almost imperceptible vibrations were passing from the interior of the tree into him; he explained this to himself without any difficulty by supposing that a wind, not otherwise noticeable and which was, perhaps, creeping over the slope close to the ground, was making itself felt in the wood, although he had to acknowledge that the trunk seemed too stout to be affected so markedly by such a slight movement of air. What interested him particularly was not, however, this idea or one of any similar kind, but he was more and more surprised, indeed impressed, by the effect produced in himself by what was passing over into him without ceasing: he felt he had never been filled with more delicate vibrations, his body was being treated in some sort like a soul, and made capable of receiving a degree of influence which could not really have been felt at all in the usual well-defined clarity of physical conditions. In addition to that, he could not, in the first moments, properly distinguish which sense it was by which he was receiving so delicate and pervading a communication; furthermore, the condition it was producing within him was so perfect and so persistent, different from all others, but so little to be represented by the heightening of anything he had ever experienced, that, for all its delicious quality, he could not think of calling it pleasure. All the same, endeavouring always to account for the least perceptible experiences, he insistently asked himself what was happening to him and almost immediately found an expression which satisfied him, as he said aloud to himself that he had reached the other side of Nature. As happens sometimes in a dream, the expression gave him pleasure, and he believed it to be almost completely apt. Everywhere and more and more regularly filled with this impulse which kept recurring in strangely interior intervals, his body became indescribably touching to him and of no other use than that he might be present in it, purely and cautiously, exactly like a ghost, already living elsewhere, that sadly enters what has already been gently laid aside, in order to belong once more, though even absent-mindedly, to a world once felt to be so indispensable. Looking round him slowly, without otherwise altering his position, he recognized everything, remembered it, smiled at it as it were with distant affection, let it be, like something known long ago, that had once, in former circumstances, been connected with him. He looked at a passing bird, a shadow attracted his attention, even the path itself, the way it went on and passed out of sight, filled him with thoughtful insight, which seemed to him so much the purer in proportion as he knew himself to be independent of it. He could not have told where his usual dwelling-place was, but that he was *returning* to all this here, was standing in this body, as if in the recess of a quitted window, looking forth—of that he was so convinced for the space of some few seconds that the sudden appearance of someone from the house would have affected him in the most painful manner; whereas he was actually quite prepared, in his nature, to see Polyxène or Raimondine, or any other of the dead belonging to the house, appearing from the turn of the path. He understood the silent superabundance of their manifestation, it was a familiar thing to him to see this fleeting, unconditional use of forms of earthly origin, the complex of their customs usurped in him the place of all that he had otherwise learnt; he was confident that, moving amongst them, he would not strike them as strange. A periwinkle standing near, whose blue gaze he had often already seen, came to him now from a more spiritual distance, but with such inexhaustible significance, as if nothing more were now to be concealed. Altogether he became aware that all objects appeared to him now more distant and at the same time, somehow or other, more true. This might be due to his own gaze, which was no longer directed forwards and dispersed out there in the open; he was looking back at things, as it were over his shoulder, and a daring, sweet flavour was added to their existence, now finished for him, as if everything had been spiced with a touch of the blossom of farewell.

Saying to himself from time to time that this could not last, he yet did not fear the cessation of this extraordinary condition, as if only such an ending could be expected of it as was, like that of music, in complete conformity with law.

All at once his position began to be uncomfortable, he felt the trunk, the weariness of the book in his hand, and he stepped forward. A wind was moving perceptibly through the leaves of the tree, it came from the sea, the bushes growing up the slope were tossed together.

Later he thought he could recall certain moments, in which the virtue of this one moment was contained, as in the seed. He recalled the time in that other southern garden (Capri), when a bird-call in the open and in his inner consciousness were one, when it did not, as it were, break on the barrier of his body, but gathered both together into an undivided space, in which there was only one region of the purest, deepest consciousness, mysteriously protected. On that occasion he had closed his eyes, so that he might not be confused by the contour of the body in such a generously granted experience, and infinity passed into him from all sides in so familiar a manner that he could believe he felt within him the gentle presence of the stars which had now appeared.

He remembered also how much it meant to him when, leaning against a fence in a similar attitude, he could see the starry heavens through the gentle branches of an olive-tree, how vision-like the world-space before him was in that disguise, or how, when he continued thus for a sufficient length of time, everything was so completely absorbed into the clear solution of his heart, that the flavour of creation was present in his being. He thought it possible that such moments of complete surrender would give food for thought as far back as in his sombre childhood; he had only to recall the passion which always seized him when it came to facing a storm, how, with his feelings in a tumult and striding over great plains, he broke through the wall of wind which met him again and again, or how, standing in the bow of a ship, he swept blindly through dense distances, which closed more densely behind him. But when, from the first, the elemental rush of the air, the pure and manifold action of the water and the heroic aspect of the moving clouds affected him beyond measure, indeed when he felt it entering into his soul, in a quite literal sense, as destiny—he who could never understand it in the human sphere—he could not fail to recognize that since the last experiences of these influences he was, as it were, finally delivered over to such relationships. A gentle something separated him from his fellows by a pure, almost apparent, intermediate space, through which it was possible to pass single items but which absorbed any relationship into itself—and, being saturated with it, intervened like a dark, deceptive vapour between himself and others. He did not know yet to what extent his separation was sensed by others. As far as he was concerned, it gave to him, for the first time, a certain freedom towards men—the small beginning of poverty, which made him lighter, gave him a peculiar ease of movement amongst these others, whose hopes were set on one another, who were burdened with cares and bound together in death and life. He still felt the temptation within him to set his ease against their heaviness, although he saw already that he deceived them by it, since they could not know that his kind of conquest had been won not (as in the case of the hero) within all their constraints, not in the heavy atmosphere of their hearts, but in a region beyond, a region having so little reference to human conditions, that they would only have called it "emptiness". The only thing by which he could address himself to them was, perhaps, his simplicity; it was reserved for him to speak to them of joy, when he found them too much involved in the opposites of happiness, and also to communicate to them something of his converse with Nature, things which they had ignored or only noticed in passing.

I   Mask of the Man with the Broken Nose

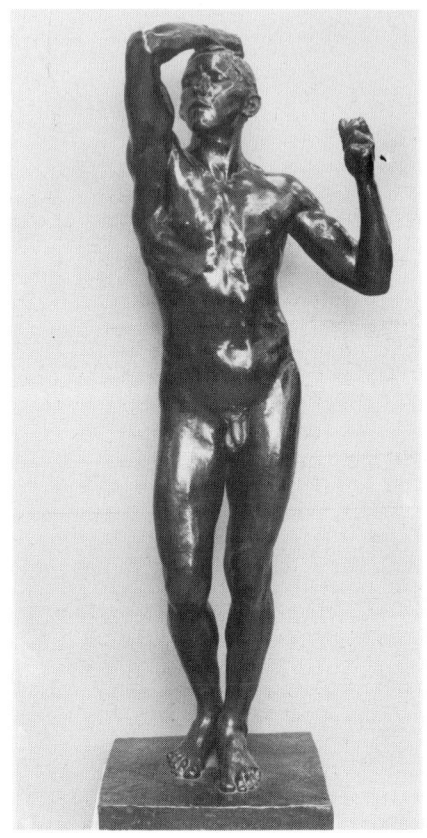

II The Age of Bronze

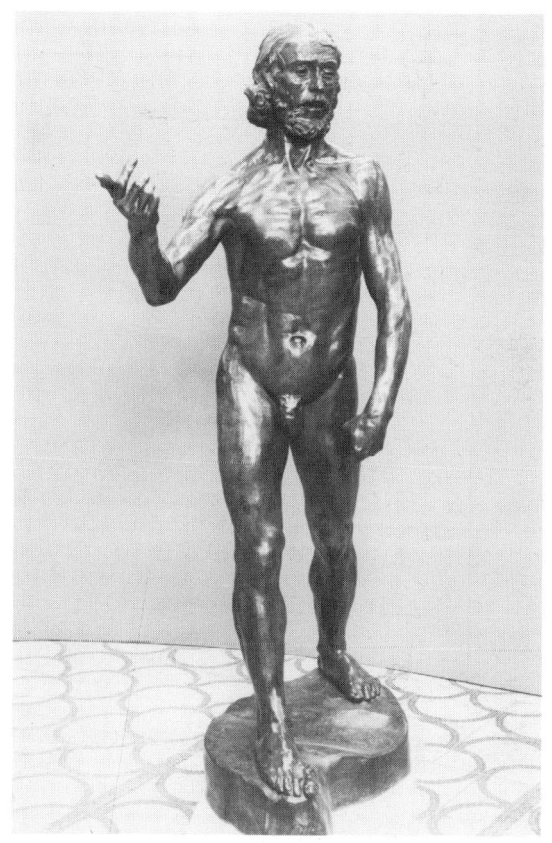

III St John the Baptist

IV The Muse, 'La Méditation'

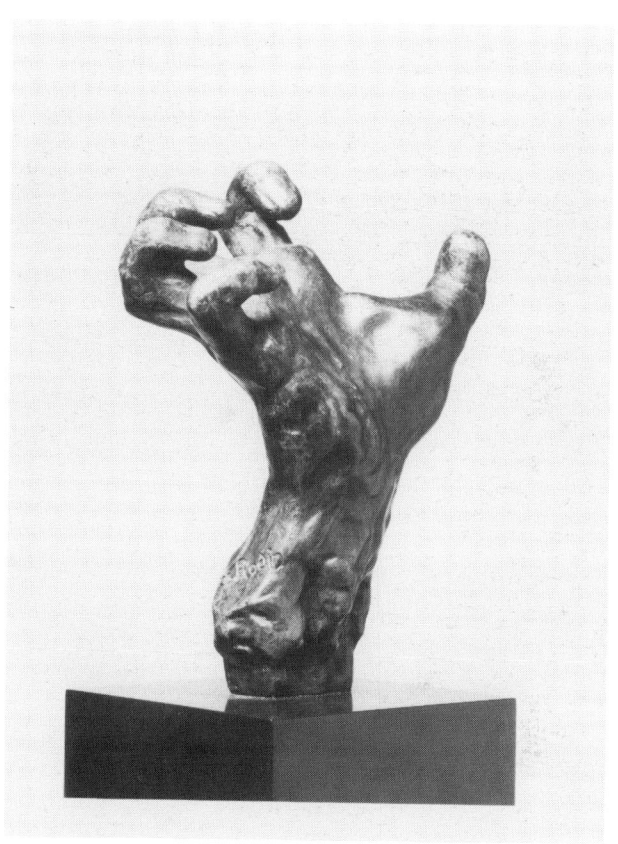

V Hand

VI The Kiss

VII The Eternal Idol

VIII   Gates of Hell

IX   The Thinker

X The Danaïd

XI   The Fallen Caryatid Carrying her Stone

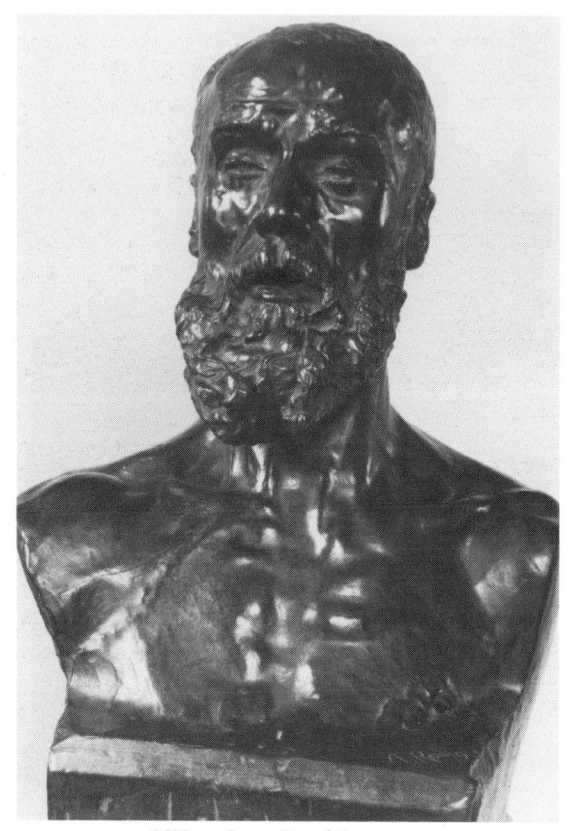

XII   Jean-Paul Laurens

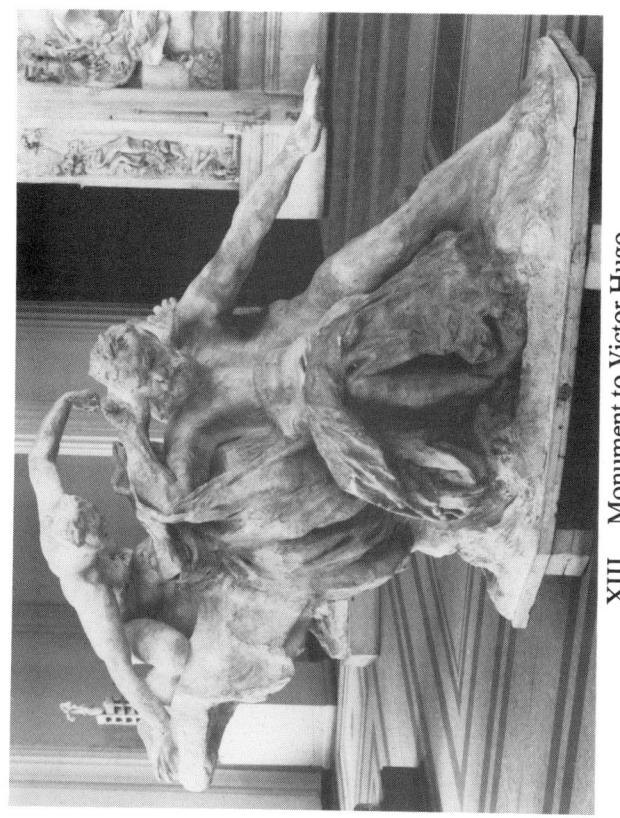

XIII Monument to Victor Hugo

XIV   Monument to Balzac

XV 'Le Guignon', illustration from *Les Fleurs du Mal*

XVI   'La Beauté', illustration from *Les Fleurs du Mal*

Note-book Entry

He had, really, been free long since, and if anything prevented his dying, it was perhaps simply the fact that he had already overlooked it at some time somewhere, so that, unlike the rest, he did not need to go forward to it, but only to go back. His life was already beyond, present in the assured things with which children play, and was perishing in them. Or it was preserved in the upward glance of a woman passing by, at any rate it remained there at its own risk. But the dogs also ran past with it, restless and looking round to see if he were not going to take it away from them. But, nevertheless, when he approached the almond-tree in full blossom, he was taken aback to find it so completely there, wholly transferred, wholly occupied there, wholly removed from himself; and he himself not sufficiently definite in the face of it and too dull even to reflect that existence of his. Had he been a saint, he would have gained from this condition a serene freedom, the infinitely irrevocable joy of poverty: for it was thus, perhaps, that Saint Francis lay, consumed and appropriated, the whole world having the flavour of his being. But he had not peeled off the Self cleanly and effectively, he had torn himself out of himself, giving away bits of the peel with it, and had often held himself to an imaginary mouth, as children do with dolls, smacking his lips, and the fragment was left lying. So that now he was like refuse lying in the way—however much sweetness there may have been in him.

Memory

I REPEAT: I find it quite comprehensible that those who have to depend entirely upon themselves, upon their own life's usefulness and bearableness, should feel a certain relief, if there is induced in them a spiritual nausea which enables them to rid themselves piece-wise of the misunderstandings and indigestible experiences of their childhood. But I? Am I not, indeed, born to form angels, things, animals, if need be, monsters, precisely in connexion with such experiences, which were beyond experiencing, were too big, too premature, too horrible? Precisely this, O my inexorable God, was what you demanded of me and called me to do, long before I was of age. And I sat up in my forlorn hospital bed, beside which lay the uniform of my cadet years, folded with meticulous care, and wrote at Thy command and knew not what I wrote. For besides Thee, my God, besides Thee, there was above me only the dull green, shaded night-light. No sooner did I, at last, leave hospital, than the most trivial contact with communal life would engulf me, it was impossible even to think of writing, not even at night in my dark bed amongst the fifty sleeping forms. A heaven of surveillance and disfavour was poured out over us all, it clung to us everywhere, and it was even something to be able to feel a kind of confiding intimacy with one's own locker in the schoolroom, as with the only friendly interior. And you, meadow playground, trampled bare, as you were, by the ferocity of play, by the impatience, the violence, and the vengeance of all these helpless boys: were you not the first meadow I ever knew? Oh! I walked over you more carefully, as if to let you recover beneath me. Had I known in those days the happy contact of bare-foot walking, I should surely have comforted you with the innocence and curiosity in the soles of my feet. For comfort seemed to me to be the one thing needed. And although I was the most miserable of all the hundred, in my daily distress, you made possible this miracle, that I sometimes found within me a grain of comfort, like pure resin, and I laid it on my gently glimmering heart and it gave forth its scent. But to write was out of the question. There was never an hour that did not echo the voice of command, and behind the childish terror of it the next command was standing ready. In the same way our going to sleep was regulated by orders, moment by moment, until we finally came under the bedclothes in a state of confusion. And then the Slovene corporal Gobec would pass along our beds and, hearing only his own footsteps as he turned off various lights, would repeat with lowered voice, as if speaking in the name of the silence and the darkness, "Lie down on the right side, say the Lord's Prayer, go to sleep——" that it was well-meant made no difference, for that too was a command. And in the morning before daybreak the malicious bugle or the reproach of the drum wrenched us out of uncomprehended sleep into unrecognizable wakefulness. Did I owe it to you, that I anticipated that? I do not know. But throughout almost the whole of one spring, long before the morning call, I used to stand alone in the empty corridor, just beginning to grow whiter, in which one simple window after another looked down on the empty space of the park, seeming not to comprehend it. A framed lithograph, which gradually grew more clearly distinguishable, hung on each of the intervening wall-spaces between them, and was far too small for the expanse between window and window. I knew these pictures were of battle-scenes—Radetsky and Spork and, higher up, always hanging a little askew, Frederick the Beautiful—and I had long known all these slim Austrian tunics, in front of whom Radetsky sat alone, square-set and short-necked, on a magnificent horse. I had often had time to study these pictures, but although I remained standing before some of them at this early hour, I fancy I did not pay much attention to them. Perhaps I was thinking of my father, for, however foreign war was to me, I still liked to think that many of our family had distinguished themselves in such activities right down to my own time; most of all I should have liked to see in each of those whom I saw there playing a valiant part, an ancestor of my own; and I was annoyed with those whom I saw half raising themselves with patient dignity in the dust beside their fallen shako, because they were not in any way connected with me. When I realized that, I moved on (if I am not mistaken) to the next window, standing and gazing out . . . and there too something very similar may well have happened. At first I saw the actual park, away beyond the wide sandy foreground: first the grounds, which were reserved for the officers, in which, contrary to all regulations, I sometimes lost myself. . . .

Some Reflections on Dolls

(*Occasioned by the wax dolls of Lotte Pritzel*)

IN order to define the sphere within which the existence of these dolls falls, one might conjecture concerning them that there are no children in their lives: this would be, in a certain sense, the condition of their origin, that the world of children was past and over. In these figures the doll has at last outgrown the understanding, the sympathy, the pleasure, and the sorrow of the child, it has become independent, grown-up, prematurely old, it has entered upon all the unrealities of its own life.

Have we not asked ourselves a thousand times anent the plump, unchanging dolls of childhood, as we do in the case of certain students, what will they be later? Are these then the grown-up versions of those doll-childhoods, which were pampered to excess by real and enacted emotions? Are these the fruits which they fleetingly reflected in humanly saturated atmosphere? The sham fruits, the germ of which knew no rest, being now almost washed away by tears, and now exposed to the arid heat of anger or to the void of forgetfulness; planted in the softest depth of a tenderness infinitely experimental and torn out again a hundred times, flung into a corner amongst sharp-edged broken objects, scorned, spurned, done with.

Fed like the "Ka" on imaginary food, when it seemed absolutely essential that they should be given real food, they messed themselves with it like spoiled children, being impenetrable and incapable of absorbing, at any point, even a drop of water in their extreme state of well-enough known solidity; without any judgment of their own, acquiescent towards every rag, and yet, once it was theirs, possessing it in their own careless, complacent, unclean manner; awake only at the moment of opening their eyes, then immediately continuing to sleep with their disproportionate, mobile eyes open, scarcely capable, indeed, of distinguishing whether it was the mechanical lid or that other thing, the air, which lay upon them; indolent, dragged about through the changing emotions of the day, remaining where they lie; made a confidant, a confederate, like a dog, not, however, receptive and forgetful like a dog, but in both cases a burden; initiated into the first, nameless experiences of their owners, lying about in their earliest uncanny lonelinesses, as in the midst of empty rooms, as if all they had to do was to exploit unfeelingly the new spaciousness with all their limbs—taken into cots, dragged into the heavy folds of illnesses, present in dreams, involved in the fatalities of nights of fever: such were these dolls. For they themselves never made any effort in all this; they lay there on the border of the children's sleep, filled, at most, with the rudimentary idea of falling down, allowing themselves to *be dreamed*; as it was their habit, during the day, to be lived unwearyingly with energies not their own.

When one thinks how grateful other things are for tender treatment, how they recover under it, indeed, how they feel even the hardest usage to be a consuming caress, provided only that they are loved, a caress which, no doubt, wears them away, but beneath which they take, as it were, courage which permeates them the more strongly, the more their body gives way (it makes them almost mortal, in a higher sense, so that they are able to share with us that grief which is our greatest possession); when we consider this and recall the sensitive beauty that certain things have been able to appropriate, which have been thoroughly and intimately incorporated in human life; I am not saying even that it is necessary to visit the rooms of the *Armeria* in Madrid and to admire the suits of armour, helmets, daggers, and two-handed swords, in which the pure, clever art of the armourer is immeasurably excelled by that something which the proud and fiery use of them has added to these weapons; I am not thinking of the smiling and the weeping which lie hidden in much-worn jewels; I do not dare to think of a certain pearl, in which the uncertain nature of its subaqueous world had gained such heightened spiritual significance that the whole inscrutability of destiny seemed to utter

SOME REFLECTIONS ON DOLLS

its lament in that innocent pearl-drop; I pass over the intimate, the touching, the deserted, thoughtful aspect of many things, which, as I passed them, moved me deeply by their beautiful participation in human living; I will only cite in passing quite simple things: a sewing clamp, a spinning-wheel, a domestic loom, a bridal glove, a cup, the binding and the leaves of a Bible; not to speak of the mighty will of a hammer, the self-surrender of a violin, the friendly eagerness of horn spectacles, —indeed, only throw that pack of cards on the table, with which patience has been played so often, and it forms at once the centre of melancholy hopes, which have long since been realized in ways not hoped for. If we were to bring all this to mind again and at the same moment to find one of these dolls —pulling it out from a pile of more responsive things—it would almost anger us with its frightful obese forgetfulness, the hatred, which undoubtedly has always been a part of our relationship to it unconsciously, would break out, it would lie before us unmasked as the horrible foreign body on which we had wasted our purest ardour; as the externally painted watery corpse, which floated and swam on the flood-tides of our affection, until we were on dry land again and left it lying forgotten in some undergrowth. I know, I know it was necessary for us to have things of this kind, which acquiesced in everything. The simplest love relationships were quite beyond our comprehension, we could not possibly have lived and had dealings with a person who *was* something; at most, we could only have entered into such a person and have lost ourselves there. With the doll we were forced to assert ourselves, for, had we surrendered ourselves to it, there would then have been no one there at all. It made no response whatever, so that we were put in the position of having to take over the part it should have played, of having to split our gradually enlarging personality into part and counterpart; in a sense, through it to keep the world, which was entering into us on all sides, at a distance. The things which were happening to us incomprehensibly we mixed in the doll, as in a test tube, and saw them there change colour and boil up. That is to say, we *invented* that also, it was so abysmally devoid of phantasy, that our imagination became inexhaustible in dealing with it. For hours together, for whole weeks we were content to lay the first downlike silk of our hearts in folds against this motionless mannequin, but I cannot help thinking that there were certain all too lengthy afternoons in which our twofold inspirations flagged, and suddenly we sat facing it, expecting something from it. It may be that there was then one of those things lying near, which are ugly and shabby by nature and consequently full of their own opinions, the head of an indestructible Casper, a half-broken horse, or something that made a noise and that could hardly wait to submerge us and the whole room by exerting its full powers. But even if this was not so; if there was nothing lying there to suggest other thoughts to us, if that creature without occupation continued, in its stupid stolidity, to put on airs, ignorant, like a peasant Danaë, of everything but the ceaseless golden rain of our inventiveness: I wish I could remember if we inveighed against it, flew into a passion and let the monster know that our patience was at an end? If, standing in front of it and trembling with rage, we did not demand to know, item by item, what actual use it was making of all these riches. It was silent then, not deliberately, it was silent because that was its constant mode of evasion, because it was made of useless and entirely irresponsible material, was silent, and the idea did not occur to it to take some credit to itself on that score, although it could not but gain great importance thereby in a world in which Destiny, and even God Himself, have become famous above all because they answer us with silence. At a time when everyone was still intent on giving us a quick and reassuring answer, the doll was the first to inflict on us that tremendous silence (larger than life) which was later to come to us repeatedly out of space, whenever we approached the frontiers of our existence at any point. It was facing the doll, as it stared at us, that we experienced for the first time (or am I mistaken?) that emptiness of feeling, that heart-pause, in which we should perish did not the whole, gently persisting Nature then lift us across abysses like some lifeless thing. Are we not strange creatures to let ourselves go and to be induced to place our earliest affections where they remain hopeless? So that everywhere there was imparted to that most spontaneous tenderness the bitterness of knowing that it was in vain? Who knows if such memories have not caused many a man afterwards, out there in life, to suspect that he is not lovable? If the influence of their doll does not continue to work disastrously in this and that person, so that they pursue vague satisfactions, simply in opposition to the state of unsatisfied desire by which it ruined their lives? I remember seeing, in the hands of the children of a manor house on a lonely Russian estate, an old inherited doll which the whole family resembled. A poet might succumb to the domination of a marionette, for the marionette has only imagination. The doll has none, and is precisely so much less than a thing as the marionette is more. But this being-less-than-a-thing, in its utter irremediability, is the secret of its superiority. The child must accustom itself to things, it must accept them, each thing has its pride. Things put up with the doll, none of them love it, we might imagine that the table throws it down, scarcely have we withdrawn our glance, before it is lying once more on the floor. Beginners in the world, as we were, we could not feel superior to any thing except, at most, to such a half-object as this, given to us the way some broken fragment is given to the creatures in aquariums, so that it may serve them as a measure and landmark in the world around them. We took our bearings from the doll. It was by nature on a lower level than ourselves, so that we could flow towards it imperceptibly, find ourselves in it and recognize our new surroundings in it, even if a little dimly. But we soon realized that we could not make a person or a thing of it, and at such moments it became a stranger to us, and all the confidences we had poured into and over it became foreign to us.

But that, in spite of all this, we did not make an idol of you, you sack, and did not perish in the fear of you, that was, I tell you, because we were not thinking of *you* at all. We were thinking of something quite different, an invisible Something, which we held high above you and ourselves, secretly and with foreboding, and for which both we and you were, so to say, merely pretexts, we were thinking of a soul: the doll-soul.

Great, courageous soul of the rocking-horse, you rocking breakers tossing the boy's heart, soul that agitated the air of the play-room until it frenzied as over the world's famous battle-fields, proud, credible, almost visible soul. How you made the walls, the cross-work of the windows, the daily horizons tremble, as though the storms of the future were already shaking these most provisional conventions, which, in the stationariness of the afternoons, could appear so invincible. Ah! how you swept one away, you rocking-horse soul, away and into the realm of the irresistibly heroic, where one perished gloriously and glowingly with one's hair in the most frightful disorder. And there you lay, doll, and had not enough innocence to understand that your St. George was rolling beneath him the beast of your stupidity, the dragon that turned the most surging tides of our emotions into a solid mass within you, into a perfidious, indifferent unbreakableness. Or you, convinced soul of the tramway, that was almost able to get the better of us when we travelled round the room, believing even only a little in our tram nature. You, souls of all these solitary games and adventures; ingenuously complaisant soul of the ball, soul in the smell of the domino pieces, inexhaustible soul of the picture book. Soul of the school satchel, towards which we felt a little distrustful because it was often so obviously on the side of the grown-ups; dumb soul of the tube of the good little trumpet: how amiable you all were and almost comprehensible. Only you, doll's soul, one could never say exactly where you really were. Whether you were in oneself or in the sleepy creature over there, whom one constantly endowed with you; undoubtedly we often relied upon one another, and in the end neither of us had you, and you were trodden under foot. When were you ever really present? On a birthday morning perhaps, when a new doll sat there and seemed almost to appropriate some bodily warmth from the still warm cake beside it? Or on the eve of Christmas, when the dolls we already possessed felt the

SOME REFLECTIONS ON DOLLS

over-ruling proximity of our future dolls through the door of the room which had been closed to us for days? Or—what is more probable—when a doll suddenly fell down and became ugly: then, for a second, it was as if you were taken off your guard. And you were, I believe, capable of giving pain as indefinite as the beginning of toothache, when we don't yet know just where it is going to be, when the favourite doll, Anna, was suddenly lost, not to be found again for ever: was gone. But fundamentally one was so busy keeping you alive that one had no time to determine what you were. I cannot say what it is like, when a little girl dies and refuses, even at the very end, to let go one of her dolls (perhaps one which had always been quite neglected), so that the poor thing is completely dry and withered in the consuming heat of her feverish hand, caught up into the Serious, the Ultimate: does a little bit of soul then form within it, curious to see a real soul?

O doll-soul, not made by God, you soul, asked for capriciously from some thoughtless fairy, thing-soul breathed forth by an idol with mighty effort, which we have all, half timidly, half magnanimously received and from which no one can entirely withdraw himself, O soul, that has never been really worn, that has only been kept always stored up (like furs in summer), protected by all kinds of old-fashioned odours: look, now the moths have got into you. You have been left untouched too long, now a hand both careful and mischievous is shaking you—look, look, all the little woebegone moths are fluttering out of you, indescribably mortal, beginning, even at the moment when they find themselves, to bid themselves farewell.

And so, in the end, we have quite destroyed you, doll-soul, whilst thinking to care for you in our dolls; they were, after all, the maggots which ate you away—that is the explanation why they were so fat and inert and why they could not be got to take any more food.

Now this new, timid race escapes and flutters through our subconscious feeling. Perceiving it, we are tempted to say that they are little sighs, so tenuous that our hearing is not sufficient for them, they appear, as they vanish, on the quiveringmost borders of our vision. For this is their only concern: to fade away. Sexless as the dolls of childhood were, they can find no decease in their stagnant ecstasy, which has neither inflow nor outflow. It is as if they were consumed with the desire for a beautiful flame, into which they might fling themselves after the manner of moths (and then the immediate smell of their burning would inundate us with limitless, hitherto unknown emotions). Reflecting thus and looking up, one is confronted and almost overwhelmed by their waxen nature.

Primal Sound

IT must have been when I was a boy at school that the phonograph was invented. At any rate it was at that time a chief object of public wonder; this was probably the reason why our science master, a man given to busying himself with all kinds of handiwork, encouraged us to try our skill in making one of these instruments from the material that lay nearest to hand. Nothing more was needed than a piece of pliable cardboard bent to the shape of a funnel, on the narrower round orifice of which was stuck a piece of impermeable paper of the kind used to seal bottled fruit. This provided a vibrating membrane, in the middle of which we then stuck a bristle from a coarse clothes brush at right angles to its surface. With these few things one part of the mysterious machine was made, receiver and reproducer were complete. It now only remained to construct the receiving cylinder, which could be moved close to the needle marking the sounds by means of a small rotating handle. I do not now remember what we made it of; there was some kind of cylinder which we covered with a thin coating of candle-wax to the best of our ability. Our impatience, brought to a pitch by the excitement of sticking and fitting the parts, as we jostled one another over it, was such that the wax had scarcely cooled and hardened before we put our work to the test.

How this was done can easily be imagined. When someone spoke or sang into the funnel, the needle in the parchment transferred the sound-waves to the receptive surface of the roll turning slowly beneath it, and then, when the moving needle was made to retrace its path (which had been fixed in the meantime with a coat of varnish), the sound which had been ours came back to us tremblingly, haltingly from the paper funnel, uncertain, infinitely soft and hesitating and fading out altogether in places. Each time the effect was complete. Our class was not exactly one of the quietest, and there can have been few moments in its history when it had been able as a body to achieve such a degree of silence. The phenomenon, on every repetition of it, remained astonishing, indeed positively staggering. We were confronting, as it were, a new and infinitely delicate point in the texture of reality, from which something far greater than ourselves, yet indescribably immature, seemed to be appealing to us as if seeking help. At the time and all through the intervening years I believed that that independent sound, taken from us and preserved outside us, would be unforgettable. That it turned out otherwise is the cause of my writing the present account. As will be seen, what impressed itself on my memory most deeply was not the sound from the funnel but the markings traced on the cylinder; these made a most definite impression.

I first became aware of this some fourteen or fifteen years after my school-days were past. It was during my first stay in Paris. At that time I was attending the anatomy lectures in the École des Beaux-Arts with considerable enthusiasm. It was not so much the manifold interlacing of the muscles and sinews nor the complete agreement of the inner organs one with another that appealed to me, but rather the bare skeleton, the restrained energy and elasticity of which I had already noticed when studying the drawings of Leonardo. However much I puzzled over the structure of the whole, it was more than I could deal with; my attention always reverted to the study of the skull, which seemed to me to constitute the utmost achievement, as it were, of which this chalky element was capable; it was as if it had been persuaded to make just in this part a special effort to render a decisive service by providing a most solid protection for the most daring feature of all, for something which, although itself narrowly confined, had a field of activity which was boundless. The fascination which this particular structure had for me reached such a pitch finally, that I procured a skull in order to spend many hours of the night with it; and, as always happens with me and things, it was not only the moments of deliberate attention which made this ambiguous object really mine: I owe my familiarity with it, beyond doubt, in part to that passing glance, with which we involuntarily examine and perceive our daily environment, when there exists any relationship at all between it and us. It was a passing glance of this kind which I suddenly checked in its course, making it exact and attentive. By candlelight—which is often so peculiarly alive and challenging—the coronal suture had become strikingly visible, and I knew at once what it reminded me of: one of those unforgotten grooves, which had been scratched in a little wax cylinder by the point of a bristle!

And now I do not know: is it due to a rhythmic peculiarity of my imagination, that ever since, often after the lapse of years, I repeatedly feel the impulse to make that spontaneously perceived similarity the starting point for a whole series of unheard of experiments? I frankly confess that I have always treated this desire, whenever it made itself felt, with the most unrelenting mistrust—if proof be needed, let it be found in the fact that only now, after more than a decade and a half, have I resolved to make a cautious statement concerning it. Furthermore, there is nothing I can cite in favour of my idea beyond its obstinate recurrence, a recurrence which has taken me by surprise in all sorts of places, divorced from any connexion with what I might be doing.

What is it that repeatedly presents itself to my mind? It is this:

The coronal suture of the skull (this would first have to be investigated) has—let us assume—a certain similarity to the closely wavy line which the needle of a phonograph engraves on the receiving, rotating cylinder of the apparatus. What if one changed the needle and directed it on its return journey along a tracing which was not derived from the graphic translation of a sound, but existed of itself naturally—well: to put it plainly, along the coronal suture, for example. What would happen? A sound would necessarily result, a series of sounds, music . . .

Feelings—which? Incredulity, timidity, fear, awe—which of all the feelings here possible prevents me from suggesting a name for the primal sound which would then make its appearance in the world . . .

Leaving that side for the moment: what variety of lines then, occurring anywhere, could one not put under the needle and try out? Is there any contour that one could not, in a sense, complete in this way and then experience it, as it makes itself felt, thus transformed, in another field of sense?

At one period, when I began to interest myself in Arabic poems, which seem to owe their existence to the simultaneous and equal contributions from all five senses, it struck me for the first time, that the modern European poet makes use of these contributors singly and in very varying degree, only one of them—sight overladen with the seen world—seeming to dominate him constantly; how slight, by contrast, is the contribution he receives from inattentive hearing, not to speak of the indifference of the other senses, which are active only on the periphery of consciousness and with many interruptions within the limited spheres of their practical activity. And yet the perfect poem can only materialize on condition that the world, acted upon by all five levers simultaneously, is seen, under a definite aspect, on the supernatural plane, which is, in fact, the plane of the poem.

A lady, to whom this was mentioned in conversation, exclaimed that this wonderful and simultaneous capacity and achievement of all the senses was surely nothing but the presence of mind and grace of love—incidentally she thereby bore her own witness to the sublime reality of the poem. But the lover is in such splendid danger just because he must depend upon the co-ordination of his senses, for he knows that they must meet in that unique and risky centre, in which, renouncing all extension, they come together and have no permanence.

As I write this, I have before me the diagram which I have always used as a ready help whenever ideas of this kind have demanded attention. If the world's whole field of experience, including those spheres which are beyond our knowledge, be represented by a complete circle, it will be immediately evident that, when the black sectors, denoting that which we are incapable of experiencing, are measured against the lesser, light sections, corresponding to what is illuminated by the senses, the former are very much greater.

Now the position of the lover is this, that he feels himself unexpectedly placed in the centre of the circle, that is to say, at the point where the known and the incomprehensible, coming forcibly together at one single point, become complete and simply a possession, losing thereby, it is true, all individual character. This position would not serve the poet, for individual variety must be constantly present for him, he is compelled to use the sense sectors to their full extent, as it must also be his aim to extend each of them as far as possible, so that his lively delight, girt for the attempt, may be able to pass through the five gardens in one leap.

As the lover's danger consists in the non-spatial character of his standpoint, so the poet's lies in his awareness of the abysses which divide the one order of sense experience from the other: in truth they are sufficiently wide and engulfing to sweep away from before us the greater part of the world—who knows how many worlds?

The question arises here, as to whether the extent of these sectors on the plane assumed by us can be enlarged to any vital degree by the work of research. The achievements of the microscope, of the telescope, and of so many devices which increase the range of the senses upwards and downwards, do they not lie in another sphere altogether, since most of the increase thus achieved cannot be interpenetrated by the senses, cannot be "experienced" in any real sense? It is, perhaps, not premature to suppose that the artist, who develops the five-fingered hand of his senses (if one may put it so) to ever more active and more spiritual capacity, contributes more decisively than anyone else to an extension of the several sense fields, only the achievement which gives proof of this does not permit of his entering his personal extension of territory in the general map before us, since it is only possible, in the last resort, by a miracle.

But if we are looking for a way by which to establish the connexion so urgently needed between the different provinces now so strangely separated from one another, what could be more promising than the experiment suggested earlier in this record? If the writer ends by recommending it once again, he may be given a certain amount of credit for withstanding the temptation to give free rein to his fancy in imagining the results of the assumptions which he has suggested.

Soglio. On the day of the Assumption of the Blessed Virgin, 1919.

The Young Poet

(Some Conjectures concerning the Birth of Poems)

STILL hesitating to distinguish between the predominant and the lesser amongst treasured experiences, I am confined to quite provisional means of expression when I attempt to describe the nature of a poet: that tremendous and child-like nature, which occurred (we do not understand how) not only in unsurpassably great figures of earlier times, but which is here also, beside us, actually mobilizing, it may be, in the boy who lifts up his great eyes and does not see us, this nature which assails young hearts, at a time when they are still powerless to face the slightest form of life, in order to fill them with capacities and relationships, which immediately exceed all that can be acquired in a whole existence; indeed, who would be able to speak calmly of this nature? Were it the case, that it did not occur any longer, that we could contemplate it at a distance in that improbable phenomenon, the poems of Homer: we should gradually formulate it, we should give to it a name and period, like the other things of the past; for what is it but the past that breaks out in the hearts which are convulsed by such forces? Here in our midst, in this multifariously modern town, in that honestly busy house, amongst the noise of vehicles and factories and the shouts of the vendors of newspapers, capacious journals filled to the brim with events, suddenly, who knows, all the effort, all the urgency, all the energy are outweighed by the appearance of the Titans in a heart still immature. Nothing vouches for it but the coldness of a boy's hand; nothing but an upward glance terrifiedly withdrawn; nothing but the indifference of this young creature, who does not talk to his brothers and who rises, as soon as he can, from meals which expose him far too long to the judgment of his family. He scarcely knows whether he still belongs to his mother: so greatly have all the proportions of his feeling altered since the irruption of the elements into his infinite heart.

O you mothers of poets. You chosen resorts of the Gods, in whose womb even the Unheard of must have been concerted. Did you hear voices in the depth of your conception, or did the Heavenly Ones communicate by signs?

I do not know how one can deny the utter wonderfulness of a world, in which the increase of what is knowingly calculated has never even broached the stores of what passes beyond all measurements. It is true, the gods have neglected no opportunity of exposing us: they let us uncover the great kings of Egypt in their tombs, and we were able to behold them in their natural corruption, to see how they were spared nothing. All the utmost achievements of those edifices and paintings led to nothing; the heavens did not become serener behind the smoke of the balsam cake, nor, apparently, did any subterranean company make use of the loaves and the concubines. Anyone who considers what wealth of purest and most tremendous ideas have here (and repeatedly) been rejected and repudiated by the incomprehensible Beings to whom they have been devoted, how could he avoid trembling for our greater future? But let him consider also, what the human heart would be, if certainty occurred at any place outside of it in all the world; ultimate certainty. How it would lose, at one blow, the tension it had developed through thousands of years, how it would remain a place worthy of praise, indeed, but one of which men would secretly tell, what it had been in former times. For truly, even the greatness of the gods depends upon their need: upon the fact that, whatever shrines may be kept for them, they are nowhere safe but in our heart. Into it they often plunge out of their sleep with their still confused plans; there they foregather in earnest counsel; there their decree is irresistible.

What do all the illusions prove, all unsatisfied burial chambers, all despoiled temples, if here, beside me, God becomes conscious of himself within a youth suddenly grown gloomy?

His parents see no future for him, his teachers think they have the clue to his unhappiness, his own mind renders the world vague to him, and his death keeps trying to find out the spot where he could be most easily broken: but so great is the carelessness of the heavenly power that it pours its waters into this undependable vessel. An hour since the most fleeting glance of his mother could comprehend his nature; now she would be unable to gauge it, though she included both resurrection and the fall of angels.

But what can a new creature do, that scarcely yet knows his own hands, without experience of his own nature, a stranger amongst the most ordinary turns of his mind, when he feels such an unheard of presence? How is he, who is obviously destined to be of a most precise nature later, to achieve his development between threats and caresses, both of which exceed the utmost effort of his unprepared powers? And it is not only that the bursting forth of greatness within him makes the heroic landscape of his feeling almost inaccessible to him: in proportion as his nature there takes control, in like measure, when he looks up, is he aware of mistrustful questions, bitter demands and curiosity in the faces he had hitherto loved in all security. In such a situation a boy might surely always go away, go forth, and be a shepherd. He might, in long speechless days and nights, enrich his confused inner world with wonderingly felt space; he might raise the crowded images in his soul to parity with the outspread stars. Oh, if only no one would try to persuade him and no one contradict him. Would you really seek to occupy the attention of *such* a one, one who is preoccupied beyond measure, prematurely occupied with an unfathomable nature?

Can we explain how he exists? The power which suddenly inhabits him finds converse and kinship in the childhood that still lingers in every corner of his heart; and now we see towards what tremendous relationships this outwardly so inadequate condition lies open. This spirit so disproportionate in its dimensions, which has no room in the consciousness of the youth, there hovers above a developed underconsciousness full of joys and frightfulnesses. Only by means of these resources, irrespective of the whole invisible-external creation, can it carry out its mighty purposes. But already it is tempted, by the pure communication of the senses of him whom it inhabits, to have dealings with the present world. And just as in the inner consciousness it finds its contact with the mightiest of hidden forces, so in things visible it is quickly and accurately served by small beckoning occasions: after all, it would be incompatible with the reticence of Nature to waken in the initiate what is truly significant otherwise than unobtrusively.

Whoever reads the Kleist letters will, according to the measure in which he understands that phenomenon, clarifying itself in thunderstorms, find the passage not unimportant which describes the arch of a certain gateway in Würzburg, one of the most timely impressions, on touching upon which genius, already tense, breaks out. Any thoughtful reader of Stifter (to think of another example) could bring himself to imagine that the inner vocation of this poetic narrator became inevitable at that moment when he first attempted, on one unforgettable day, to bring nearer to him, by means of a telescope, some far distant spot in the landscape, and then experienced within his utterly bewildered vision a flight of spaces, of clouds, of objects, a shock of such richness that within these seconds his spirit, openly taken by surprise, received world as Danaë received the outpoured Zeus.

Ultimately, all poetic resolution may have realized itself unexpectedly by just such incidental causes, not only when it took possession of a temperament for the first time, but repeatedly, at every turn of a nature which was fulfilling itself artistically.

Who can name you all, you confederates of inspiration, you who are no more than sounds or bells that cease, or wonderfully new bird-voices in the neglected woods, or shining light thrown by an opening window out into the hovering morning; or cascading water; or air; or glances. Chance glances of passers-by, upward glances of women sewing by the window, down to the unspeakably troubled looking-about-them of crouching, anxious dogs, so close to the expression of schoolchildren. What agreed purpose of calling forth greatness informs the most trivially commonplace! Events, so negligible that they would not be capable of deflecting the most yielding of destinies by a ten thousandth degree—behold: they beckon here, and the divine line passes over them into the eternal.

The poet, with increasing insight into his limitless tasks, will undoubtedly attach himself to what is greatest; where he finds it, it will delight or humble him, according to his choice. But the signal for the rising will be given willingly by a messenger who does not know what he is doing. It is unthinkable that the poet should regulate himself from the very start by what is great, since he is, indeed, destined to reveal himself through it, his ever present goal, by ways still indescribably peculiar to him. And how should it really have first become known to him, since it was present in his original surroundings, masked perhaps, disguising itself, or scorned, like the saint living in the intervening space under the stairs? But if it lay before him, openly revealed, in its assured, disregardful glory,—would he not then, like Petrarch, be compelled, at the sight of the countless vistas seen from the mountain he had climbed, to flee back to the ravines of his own soul, which are of inexpressibly greater concern to him, although he will never explore their depths, than that foreign region which might, at need, be explored?

Alarmed within by the distant thunder of the god, bewildered from without by an irresistible excess of appearances, the object of such violent treatment has only just room to stand on the narrow space between two worlds, until suddenly a neutral little event inundates his monstrous condition with innocence. This is the moment which places the great poem in the scales, in the one tray of which there rests his heart, overburdened with infinite responsibilities, the great poem producing the sublimely tranquillized balance.

The great poem. As I say it, it becomes clear to me that I have accepted it, until quite recently, as something which certainly exists, putting it highhandedly beyond any suspicion of coming into being. Even if the originator behind it were to appear, I should not be able to imagine the power which all *at once* had broken so great a silence. Just as the builders of the cathedrals shot up, like grains of seed, immediately and without residue, into growth and blossom in their work, which stood there as if it had always been, no longer explicable as deriving from them: so the great poets of the past and the present remain entirely incomprehensible to me, the place of each being taken by the tower and bell of his heart. Only since a most proximate younger generation, striving upward and into the future, has embodied, not insignificantly, their own growth in the growth of their poems, does my eye seek to recognize, alongside of their achievement, the circumstances of the creative personality. But even now, when I must acknowledge that poems are formed, I am far from thinking them invented; it seems to me rather as if there appeared in the soul of the poetically inspired a spiritual predisposition, which was already present between us (like an undiscovered constellation).

If we consider what admirable achievement even now stands surety for some of those who have recently entered upon their thirties, we might almost hope that they would soon, by the masterly quality of their work, make everything, which in the last thirty years has called forth our admiration, appear but the preparation for the fulfilment which their work achieves. It is clear that the most diverse circumstances must combine favourably, if such a resolute achievement is to be possible. If we examine these circumstances, the outward ones are so numerous, that in the end we give up the attempt to penetrate to those within. The excited curiosity and tireless ingenuity of an age, emancipated from a hundred inhibitions, penetrates into every secret corner of the mind and, without effort, floats out on its spate of waters creations of the mind which the individual, in whom they lay hidden, once brought slowly and painfully to the light of day. Too well practised in insight to pause, this age suddenly finds itself at landlocked waters, where, perhaps, no age has ever been without divine pretext, and in full publicity; exploring everywhere, it turns workshops into exhibition grounds and has no objection to taking its meals amongst the stores. It may be right, for it derives from the future. It occupies our minds in a manner in which no age has, for a long time, occupied those inhabiting it; it pushes and displaces and makes a clearance, each of us has much for which to thank it. And yet who has not watched it, at least for a moment, with mistrust; and asked himself if it is really concerned with fruitfulness, or only with a mechanically better and more exhaustive exploitation of the soul? It confuses us with ever new possibilities of perception; but how much has it put before us which has caused no corresponding progress in our inner life? Now I will assume that it offered, at the same time, to our determined youth the most unexpected means of gradually giving outward, visible form in precise equivalents to their purest inner realities; indeed, I am prepared to believe it possesses these means in the highest degree. But, whilst I hold myself ready to attribute to it, our age, various new artistic gains, my admiration passes on and beyond to the poems, which remain always, now no less than before, incomprehensible.

Even if there were not one amongst the younger poets who did not rejoice to profit in his outlook by the daring and intensified spirit of our time, I should, indeed, not be afraid of having treated too seriously the question of the poetic nature and the manner of its effect in the life within. All simplifications, however penetrating, do not take effect in that region where the difficult rejoices that it is difficult. After all, what can alter the situation of one who, from his early days, has been destined to set in motion supreme forces within his own heart, forces which others hold at bay in theirs and reduce to silence? And what kind of peace could be imagined for him when, within, he is suffering the assault of his god?

Concerning the Poet

THE position of the Poet in the existing world, his "meaning", was once shown to me in a fine similitude. It was on board the large sailing vessel in which we crossed from the island of Philæ to the wide stretching dams. We went up stream at first and the oarsmen had to exert themselves. I had them all facing me, sixteen of them, if I remember rightly, four in each row, two on the right oar and two on the left. Occasionally one caught the eye of one or other, but mostly their eyes saw nothing, their open gaze going out into the air, or their eyes were simply points where the hot vitality of these men lay bare, set in their metallic bodies. But sometimes, looking up quickly, one could catch one of them deep in thought, meditating on the strange disguised phenomenon facing him and on possible situations which might disclose its nature; when noticed, he immediately lost his strenuously thoughtful expression, for a moment all his feelings were in confusion, then, as quickly as he could, he reverted to the watchful gaze of an animal, until the beautiful serious expression became again the usual silly *backshish* face, with its foolish readiness to assume any required humiliating distortion of thanks. This degradation, for which travellers have long been to blame, is generally accompanied by its own penalty, in that the native seldom fails to gaze over and beyond the stranger with a look of deep hatred, lit by a gleam of understanding with the man on the far side of him. I had observed the old man, who was sitting there crouched at the end of the boat, repeatedly. His hands and feet had come into the closest association, and the pole of the rudder moved between them, guided and checked by them. His body, clad in dirty rags, was not worth mentioning, his face, beneath its disreputable turban cloth, was folded in on itself like the parts of a telescope, its extreme flatness seeming to make the eyes ooze moisture. God knows what was in the man, he looked capable of turning one into something repulsive; I should have liked to scrutinize his face, but when I turned round he was as close to me as my own ear, and to attempt to examine him at such short distance seemed too obvious a proceeding. Moreover, the spectacle of the broad river flowing towards us, the beautiful region lying constantly before us, as it were, whilst we penetrated into it, was so worthy of undivided attention and so satisfying in its effect that I ceased to occupy myself with the old man, and instead came to observe with increasing delight the movements of the boys, which, for all their vigour and effort, lost nothing of their ordered rhythm. Their rowing was now so strenuous that those at the end of the great oars rose completely from their seats each time they reached forward and, placing one leg against the seat in front of them, threw themselves back violently, the eight oar blades driving forward in the current below. At the same time they gave voice to a kind of counting in order to keep in time, but so exacting was their work that their voices frequently failed them; often they had simply to suffer such a gap, but at times an unpredictable intervention, felt by all of us in a most peculiar manner, not only helped them rhythmically, but quite perceptibly transformed the powers within them, as it were, so that, being eased, they brought fresh, still untouched sources of strength into play: just as a child, after whetting its appetite in the eating of an apple, will begin to eat afresh, radiant with enjoyment, when it discovers that the side it has been holding is still intact even to the skin.

Now I cannot postpone any longer mention of the man sitting at the front on the right-hand side of the boat. I ended by believing that I could feel in advance when his song was about to begin, but I may have been mistaken. He sang suddenly, at quite irregular intervals, and by no means always when exhaustion increased; on the contrary, his song occurred more than once when all of the rowers were vigorous or even exuberant, but even then it was the right thing; even then it was appropriate. I do not know to what extent the mood of our crew communicated itself to him; they were all behind him, he rarely looked backwards, and was not affected when he did so.

What did seem to influence him was the pure movement of his feeling when it met the open distance, in which he was absorbed in a manner half melancholy, half resolute. In him the forward thrust of our vessel and the force opposed to us were continually held in counterpoise—from time to time a surplus accumulated: then he sang. The boat overcame the opposition; but what could not be overcome (was not susceptible of being overcome) he, the magician, transmuted into a series of long floating sounds, detached in space, which each appropriated to himself. Whilst those about him were always occupied with the most immediate actuality and the overcoming of it, his voice maintained contact with the farthest distance, linking us with it until we felt its power of attraction.

I do not know how it happened, but suddenly, in this phenomenon, I understood the position of the poet, his place and effect within time, and that one might well dispute his right to every other position but this. This one, though, must be allowed to him.

The Young Workman's Letter

SOME poems of yours were read at a meeting of ours last Thursday, Mr. V., I can't forget it; I can think of no better way than to put down for you what is in my mind, as well as I can.

The day after the reading of the poems, I happened by chance to attend a Christian gathering, and perhaps that was really what put the match to the fire, causing such commotion and urgency that I write to you with all the energy and powers that I possess. It is a tremendous act of violence to begin anything. I am not able to *begin*. I simply skip what should be the beginning. Nothing is so powerful as silence. It would never have been broken, if we had not, each of us, been born into the midst of talk.

Mr. V., I am not going to speak about the evening when we heard your poetry. I am going to speak of the other evening. I am compelled to say: Who, yes—I cannot express it any other way at present, *who* then is this Christ, who interferes in everything—who knew nothing about us, nothing of our work, nothing of our needs, nothing of our joy, as we do it, suffer it, and experience it—and who yet, as it seems, constantly demands that he shall have first place in our lives? or has that just been put into his mouth? What does he want of us? He wants to help us, they say. Yes, but he behaves in a strangely helpless fashion when near us. His conditions were so entirely different. Or do the conditions not really matter, supposing he came into my room here—or into the factory there—would everything at once be different, right? Would the heart in me beat high and, so to say, continue on a different level, always going out to him? My feeling tells me that he *cannot* come. That it has no sense. Our world is not only outwardly different, it offers him no access. He would not *appear* through a ready-made coat, it is not true, he would not *show*. It was no accident that he went about in a robe without seam, and it is my belief, that the core of light in him, that made him shine so strongly, day and night, has long since been dissolved and differently dispersed. But if he was so great, this is, to my thinking, the least that we could demand of him, that in some way he should have been absorbed without residue, entirely without residue, leaving no trace. . . .

I cannot conceive that the *cross* should *remain*, which was, after all, only a cross-roads. It certainly should not be stamped on us on all occasions like a brand-mark. For is the situation not *this*: he intended simply to provide the loftier tree, on which we could ripen better. He, on the cross, is this new tree in God, and we were to be warm, happy fruit, at the top of it.

We should not always talk of what was *formerly*, but the *afterwards* should have begun. This tree, it seems to me, should have become so one with us, or we with it, and *by* it, that we should not need to occupy ourselves continually with it, but simply and quietly with God, for his aim was to lift us up and into God more purely.

When I say: God, that is a great conviction in me, not something learnt. It seems to me, the whole creation speaks this word, without reflection, though often out of a deep thoughtfulness. If this Christ has helped us to say it more fully, more effectually, with a clearer voice, so much the better, but now at last leave him out of the question. Do not always force us back into the labour and sorrow that it cost him to "redeem" us, as you put it. Let us, at last, enter into this state of redemption. Otherwise the situation of the Old Testament is certainly better, it is full of pointers towards God, wherever you open it, and when one is heavy, one falls right into the middle of God there. And once I tried to read the Koran; I did not get far, but I understood this much: it too is a mighty pointer, and God stands as the end towards which it points, in his eternal rising, in an East without end. Christ surely wanted the same thing. To point. But the people here have been like dogs, that do not understand the pointing finger and think they are meant to snap at the hand. Instead of setting out from the place of the cross-roads where this sign was high and lifted up into the night of his sacrifice, instead of proceeding onwards from this place of the cross, Christianity has settled down there and claims that it is living there in Christ, although there was no room in him, not even for his mother, nor for Mary Magdalene, as there never is room in anyone who points the way, who is a gesture and not a dwelling-place. And so they do not dwell in Christ, these stubborn of heart, who continually bring him back again and live from the setting up of a cross which stands crooked or completely blown down. They have on their conscience this concourse and standing about on the over-crowded place, it is their fault that the journey does not begin to follow the direction of the arms of the cross. They have made a *métier* out of Christian living, a bourgeois occupation, *sur place*, a pool which is alternately emptied and filled. Everything that they do of themselves, in harmony with their insuppressible nature (in so far as they are still alive), is a contradiction of this strange situation, and so they muddy their own waters and have to renew them constantly. In their zeal, they do not hesitate to make this life, which should be an object of desire and trust for us, bad and worthless—and so they hand over the earth more and more to those who are ready to gain at least temporary and quickly won profit from it, vain and suspect as it is, and no good for anything better. This increasing exploitation of life, is it not a result of the century-old denial of the worth of this world? What folly to direct our thoughts to a Beyond, when we are surrounded here by tasks and expectations and future prospects! What deceit to misappropriate pictures of present delight in order to sell them behind our backs to heaven! Oh! the impoverished earth ought long ago to have called in all these loans which have been drawn on its happiness, so that the Hereafter might be adorned with them. Does death really become less opaque because these lighting devices have been dragged into place behind it? And, since a vacuum cannot persist, will not all that has been taken away from earth be replaced by sham—is this the reason why the cities are so full of ugly artificial light and noise, because true radiance and song have been delivered over to a Jerusalem to be inhabited later? Christ may have been right to speak ill of earthly things in an age full of stale and denuded gods, although it is an insult to God (I cannot think otherwise) not to see in what is granted and permitted to us here something completely capable of making us happy to the very limit of our senses, if only we use it with precision. The *right use* is the thing. To take a good hold of this life, with warm affection and wonder, as our sole possession in the meantime; this is also—to use a homely expression—God's great "direction for use", *this* it was which Saint Francis of Assisi thought to write down in his song to the Sun, which was more glorious to him as he lay dying than was the cross, which only stood there *to point into* the sun. But what is called the Church had grown, in the meantime, to such a confusion of voices, that the song of the dying man, drowned on all sides, was heard only by a few simple monks, and infinitely confirmed by the landscape of his lovely valley. How often must such attempts have been made, to bring about a reconciliation between that Christian renunciation and the obvious friendliness and cheerfulness of the Earth. But in other ways also, within the Church, even in its very crown, earthly life achieved its own fullness and its inherent luxuriance. Why does the Church not boast that it was sufficiently vigorous not to collapse under the living weight of certain popes, whose throne was encumbered with bastard offspring, courtesans and the assassin's victims? Was there not in them more Christianity than in the fleshless restorers of the Gospels— that is to say, living, irrepressible, transforming Christianity? I mean, we do not know *what* will come of the great teachings, we must only allow them to stream forth and follow their course, and not be alarmed when they suddenly pour into the disrupted parts of life, rolling through indiscernible beds underground.

I worked in Marseilles once for some months. It was an important time for me, I owe a lot to it. Chance brought me into contact with a young painter who remained my friend until his death. He had lung trouble and had just come back from Tunis. We were a lot together, and, because the end of my contract coincided with his return to Paris, we were able to arrange to spend a few days in Avignon. I have never forgotten them. Partly because of the town itself, its buildings and its surroundings, but also because my friend, in those days of uninterrupted and somehow more intimate intercourse, told me many things, particularly about his *inner* life, with that eloquence which, it seems, is peculiar to such sufferers at certain times. Everything he said had a strangely prophetic force; through all that he poured out, often in almost breathless talks, one saw, so to say, the bottom, the stones on the bottom . . . I mean by that, something more than merely what is in us,—Nature herself, her oldest and hardest core, with which we come in contact at so many places and upon which we are, probably, dependent at moments of greatest urgency, its falling gradient determining our inclination. Furthermore, he had an unexpected and happy love affair, his heart was in an unusually exalted state, for days together, and so, by contrast, the playing fountain of his life shot up to a considerable height. To view a remarkable town and a more than pleasing landscape in the company of one in such a state is a rare privilege; and so, when I look back, those tender and at the same time passionate days of spring seem to me to be the only holidays that I have ever known in all my life. The time was so ridiculously short; for anyone else it would only have sufficed for a few impressions,—to me, unaccustomed as I am to having holidays, it seemed long. Indeed, it seems almost wrong to call that *time* which was rather a new-found state of liberty, felt purely as *space*, a being surrounded by open space, not the passing of anything. During those days I recovered childhood, if one may put it that way, a bit of early youth, all of which I had never had time to realize in myself; I looked, I learnt, I understood,—and from those days originates also the experience that it was so easy, so true, so—as my friend would have expressed it—so unproblematically simple for me to say "God". How could this house, which the popes erected for themselves there, appear otherwise than mighty to me? I had the feeling that there could not be any space inside it, but that it must be built simply of solid blocks, as if the exiles had only been concerned to pile up upon the scales of history the weight of the Papacy, its weighty ascendancy. And, in truth, this ecclesiastical palace is reared above the antique torso of a Herakles, which was built into the rocky foundations—"is it not," said Peter, "as if it had grown up in monstrous fashion from that grain of seed?"—I could much more easily understand that *this* was Christianity, in one of its many transformations, than recognize its strength and flavour in that tisane, weaker with every brew, of which it is asserted that it is prepared from the earliest and most delicate leaves.

Even the cathedrals are not the embodiment of that spirit which we are now asked to believe is the actual Christian spirit. I could imagine the fallen image of a Grecian goddess to be lying under some of them; so much florescence, so much life has blossomed in them, in spite of the fact that they soared away from that hidden body, as with a fear characteristic of their age, into the heavens which the sound of their great bells was to keep continually open.

After I returned from Avignon I went into a great many churches, in the evening and on Sundays—alone at first . . . afterwards. . . .

I have a sweetheart, scarcely more than a child, who works at home, so that she is often in a bad way when work is slack. She is a clever worker, and could easily get into a factory, but she is afraid of the boss. Her idea of liberty is boundless. It will not surprise you that she thinks of God, too, as a sort of boss, as the chief boss, as she said to me, laughingly, but with such terror in her eyes. It was a long time before she decided to go with me one evening to St. Eustache, where I liked to go because of the music of the May services. Once we got as far as Maux and looked at the tombstones in the church there. Gradually she noticed that God leaves people alone in the churches, that he makes no demand; one could imagine he was not there at all, don't you think?—but yet at the very moment when one is about to say that he is not in the church, said Martha, something holds you back. Perhaps only what human beings themselves have brought into this lofty, peculiarly intensified atmosphere through so many centuries. And perhaps it is only that the vibration of the powerful, sweet music can never quite get away; indeed, it must long since have penetrated into the stones, and these pillars and arches must be wonderfully agitated stone, and although a stone is hard and difficult to penetrate, in the end it must be deeply affected by ever recurring singing and these assaults of the organ, these onslaughts, these gales of song, every Sunday, these hurricanes on the great Feast Days. A dead calm, that is what reigns, in a special sense, in old churches. I said so to Martha. A dead calm. We listened, she understood at once, she is by nature wonderfully prepared. After that, we often went in, here and there, when we heard singing, and then we stood there close to one another. It was best of all, when a glass window was in front of us, one of those old, pictured windows, with a number of divisions, each completely filled with figures, large-sized people and small towers and all sorts of events. Nothing was too strange for them— there are castles and battles and the hunt, and the beautiful white deer appears again and again set in glowing red and burning blue. I was once given a very old wine to drink. That was what these windows are for the eye, only that the wine was simply dark red in the mouth—but this here is the same in blue also and in violet and in green. There is, indeed, absolutely *everything* in the old churches, no shyness about anything, as there is in the new churches, where only good examples appear, so to say. Here there is also what is bad and evil and terrible; what is deformed, and in want, what is ugly and unjust; and one would be inclined to say that it is, in some sort, held in love for God's sake. Here is the angel that does not exist, and the devil that does not exist; and man, who does exist, is between them, and, I can't help it, their unreality makes him more real to me. I can put together better in there what I feel when they say "a man" than I can in the street amongst people, who have nothing whatever about them that you can recognize. But that is difficult to express. And what I want to say now is still more difficult to put into words. As regards the "boss", the power (this became clear to me in there, too, very gradually, as we stood quite lost in the music), there is only *one* means of dealing with it: to go further than it does. I mean in this way: one should endeavour to see in every power claiming a right over us all power, the whole of power, power in essence, the power of God. One should say to oneself, there is only *one* power, and should understand the trivial, false, imperfect kind of power as if it were that which claims us rightly. Would it not become innocuous in this way? If one always saw in every kind of power, even in that which is evil and mischievous, power itself, I mean that which has, in the last resort, the right to be powerful, would one not then survive unharmed, so to say, even by what is unjust and despotic? Is this not precisely how we stand in relationship to all the great unknown forces? We do not experience any one of them in its purity. We accept each of them with its faults, which perhaps fit in with our faults. But, in the experience of all scholars, discoverers, and inventors, has not the assumption that they are working with great powers led them suddenly to the greatest? I am young and there is a great deal of rebellion in me; I cannot say that I act according to my understanding in every case, when impatience and disgust get the better of me—but in my heart of hearts I know that submission gets you further than resistance; it puts to shame the usurpation of power and it adds indescribably to the glory of the right kind of power. He who resists withdraws himself forcibly from the attraction of one centre of power, and he may, perhaps, succeed in leaving the field of its activity, but beyond it he finds himself in emptiness and has to look round for another force of gravitation to attract him. And this latter is generally even less legitimate than the former. So why not see, at once, in that force, within which we find ourselves, the greatest of all, without heeding its weaknesses and fluctuations? At one point or another despotic power will, of itself, come up against law, and we conserve our strength when we leave it to learn its own lesson. Of course that is one of those slow and lengthy processes which are in such complete contradiction to the remarkable upheavals of our time. But, alongside of the most rapid movements, there will always be slow ones, such, indeed, as are of so extreme a leisureliness that we shall not live to see the course they take. But that is what humanity is for, is it not, to await the realization of that which exceeds a single life-span?—From its point of view the slowest process is often the quickest, that is to say, we find that we called it slow simply because it could not be measured.

Now it seems to me there is something which is absolutely immeasurable, and men are never tired of making the mistake of bringing to it their yard-measures, mensurations and devices. And here, in the love which, with an intolerable mixture of contempt, desire, and curiosity, they call "sensual", here indeed are to be found the worst results of that vilification of earthly life which Christianity has felt obliged to engage in. Here everything is distorted and disowned, although it is from this deepest of all events that we come forth, and have ourselves the centre of our ecstasies in it. It seems to me, if I may say so, more and more incomprehensible that a doctrine which puts us in the wrong in *that* matter, where the whole creation enjoys its most blissful right, should be able, if not anywhere to prove its validity, at least to assert itself over a wide area.

Here again I think of the animated conversations which I had at that time with my departed friend, in the meadows of the Barthelasse Island in the spring and later. Even in the night before his death (he died the following afternoon a little after five o'clock) he opened up to me such pure vistas into a realm of the blindest suffering, that my life seemed to me to begin afresh at a thousand points, and when I tried to answer, I had no command of my voice. I did not know that there are tears of joy. I wept my first, like a beginner, into the hands of the friend who was dead the next day, and felt how the tide of life in Peter rose once more and overflowed as those hot drops were added to it. Am I being extravagant? I am speaking of a *too much*.

Why, I ask you, Mr. V., when people want to help us, who are so often helpless, why do they leave us in the lurch just there, at the root of all experience? Anyone who would stand by us *there* could rest satisfied that we should ask nothing further from him. For the help which he imparted to us there would grow of itself with our life, becoming, together with it, greater and stronger. And would never fail. Why are we not set in the midst of what is most mysteriously ours? How we have to creep round about it and get into it in the end; like burglars and thieves, we get into our own beautiful sex, in which we lose our way and knock ourselves and stumble and finally rush out of it again, like men caught transgressing, into the twilight of Christianity. Why, if guilt or sin had to be invented because of the inner tension of the spirit, why did they not attach it to some other part of our body, why did they let it fall on that part, waiting till it dissolved in our pure source and poisoned and muddied it? Why have they made our sex homeless, instead of making it the place for the festival of our competency?

Very well, I will allow that it should not belong to us, who are not able to answer for and administer such inexhaustible bliss. But why do we not belong to God from *this* point?

A churchman would point out to me that there is marriage, although he is not unaware of the state of affairs in respect of that institution. It does not help either to put the will to propagation within the sphere of grace—my sex is not directed only towards posterity, it is the secret of my own life—and it is only, it seems, because it may not occupy the central place there, that so many people have thrust it to the edge, and thereby lost their balance. What good is it all? The terrible untruthfulness and uncertainty of our age has its roots in the refusal to acknowledge the happiness of sex, in this peculiarly mistaken guilt, which constantly increases, separating us from the rest of Nature, even from the child, although his, the child's innocence, as I learnt in that unforgettable night, does not consist at all in the fact that he does not know sex, so to say— "but," said Peter almost inaudibly, "that incomprehensible happiness, which awakens for us at *one* place deep within the pulp of a close embrace, is still present anonymously in every part of his body." In order to describe the peculiar situation of our sensual appetite we should have to say: Once we were children in every part, now we are that in one part only. But if there were only one among us for whom this was a certainty and who was capable of providing proof of it, why do we allow it to happen that generation after generation awakens to consciousness beneath the rubble of Christian prejudices and moves like the seemingly dead in the darkness, in a most narrow space between sheer abnegations!?

Herr V., I write and write. Nearly a whole night has gone on this. I must be brief—— Have I said that I am employed in a factory? I work in the office, sometimes I have a machine to look after too. Before that, I was once able to study for a short while. Well, I only want to say how I feel. I want, you see, to be employable in relation to God, just as I am; what I do here, my work, I want to go on with it in his direction, without having my stream interrupted, if I may put it so, not even through Christ, who was once the water for many. God, on the other hand, I have the feeling that I can bring my machine to him and its first fruits, or my whole work, it enters into him without any trouble. Just as it was once an easy thing for the shepherds to bring a lamb or the fruit of the fields or their finest grapes to the gods of their life.

You see, Herr V., I have been able to write this long letter without once needing the word faith. For that seems to me to be a complicated and difficult matter, and not my affair. I won't let myself be made out bad for the sake of Christ, but I want to be good for God. I won't be addressed, as a matter of course, as a sinner, perhaps I am not one. I have such pure mornings. I could talk with God, I do not need anyone to help me to compose letters to him.

I know your poems only from the public reading of them the other evening, I have only a few books, most of them dealing with my occupation. It is true there are a few about Art and History, just what I could afford. But your poems—you must accept the fact—have occasioned this commotion in me. My friend said once: Give us teachers who will praise the present for us. You *are* such a teacher.

The Lay of the
Love and Death of
Cornet Christoph Rilke

Written 1899

". . . . on the 24 November 1663 Otto von Rilke/of Langenau/Gränitz and Ziegra/was enfeoffed at Linda with that portion of the estate of Linda left by his brother Christoph, fallen in battle in Hungary; he was required, however, to enter into a deed of reversion,/according to which the enfeoffment should be null and void/in the event of the return of the said brother Christoph (who, according to the death-certificate produced, had died as a Cornet in the Freiherr von Pirovano's Company of the Imperial Austrian Heyster Regiment of Horse) . . ."

Riding, riding, riding, through the day, through the night, through the day.

Riding, riding, riding.

And courage has grown so weary, and desire so great. No more hills to be seen, scarcely a tree. Nothing dares to stand upright. Unfamiliar cottages crouch thirstily beside the trampled wells. No sight of a tower anywhere. And ever the same unchanging scene. One has two eyes too many. Only in the night sometimes does the way seem familiar. Perhaps we go back again each night over the ground we have gained with so much effort beneath the foreign sun? Perhaps. The sun is strong, like ours at the height of summer. But it was summer when we said farewell. The women's dresses shone lingeringly out of the green. And we have been riding for long now. So it must be autumn. At least there, where sorrowing women think on us.

※ ※ ※

Von Langenau stirs in his saddle and says: "My Lord Marquis. . . ."

His neighbour, the elegant little Frenchman, had talked and laughed during the first three days. Now he is oblivious of everything. He is like a child wanting to sleep. His fine white lace collar is covered with dust and he does not notice it. Slowly he droops in his velvet saddle.

But von Langenau smiles and says: "You have strange eyes, my Lord Marquis. You must favour your mother. . . ."

At that, the youngster revives and brushes the dust from his collar and is like a new man.

※ ※ ※

Someone is talking about his mother. Obviously a German. He places his words slowly and distinctly. Like a girl making a posy, and thoughtfully trying one flower after another, not knowing what the whole will be like in the end—so he places his words. For joy? For sorrow? We are all listening. Even the spitting ceases. For these are all gentlemen who know what is seemly. And anyone in the troop who is ignorant of German, all at once understands and feels the isolated words: "At night" ... "was small" ...

※ ※ ※

Now they are all united in one common feeling, these gentlemen from France and from Burgundy, from the Low Countries, from the valleys of Carinthia, from the fortresses of Bohemia and from the Emperor Leopold. For what one of them is telling has been the experience of all and just in the same way. As if there were but *one* mother. . . .

※ ※ ※

And so they ride on into the evening, into any evening. They are silent again, but the shining words go with them. Then the Marquis takes off his helmet. His dark hair is soft and falls on his neck like a woman's, when he bends his head. And now von Langenau sees: in the distance something rising up into the radiance, something slender, dark. A solitary, half-ruined column. And later, long after they have left it behind, it occurs to him that it was a Madonna.

※ ※ ※

Camp-fire. They sit round it and wait. Wait for someone to sing. But they are too tired. The red light is heavy. It lies on the dusty boots. It creeps up to the knees, it peers into the folded hands. It is wingless. Their faces are dark. Yet, for a moment, the eyes of the little Frenchman shine with their own light. He has kissed a little rose, and now he puts it to wither again on his breast. Von Langenau has seen it, for he is not able to sleep. He thinks, I have no rose, none.

Then he sings. It is an old, sad song, which the girls at home sing in the fields, in autumn, when the harvest is ending.

✶ ✶ ✶

The little Marquis says, "You are very young, Sir?"
And von Langenau, half in sorrow and half in defiance: "Eighteen." Then they are silent.
Later, the Frenchman asks: "Have you too a sweetheart at home, Herr Junker?"
"Have you?" retorts von Langenau.
"She is fair like you."
And they are silent again, until the German exclaims: "Then why, in the devil's name, do you sit in the saddle and ride through this cursèd country to meet the Turkish dogs?"
The Marquis smiles. "So that I may return."
And von Langenau is sad. He is thinking of a fair-haired girl, with whom he used to play. Wild games. He longs to go home, for a moment only, only long enough to say the words: "Magdalena—forgive me that I was always like *that*!"
What—was? thinks the young officer.—And they have gone far.

✶ ✶ ✶

One day, in the morning, a horseman appears, and then a second, four, ten. Clad in iron, huge. Then a thousand behind them: the Army.
It is time to part.
"Safe return home, my Lord Marquis——"
"May the Virgin protect you, Herr Junker."

And they cannot part from one another. All at once they are friends, brothers. Have more to confide to one another, for they already know so much the one about the other. They hesitate. And all about them is haste and the sound of horses' hooves. Then the Marquis draws off the great gauntlet from his right hand. He takes out the little rose, plucks a petal from it. Like the breaking of the Host.

"That will protect you. Farewell."

Count von Langenau is taken aback. He gazes after the Frenchman a long time. Then he thrusts into his tunic the rose-leaf, by right another's. And it rises and falls on the waves of his heart. Bugle-call. He rides to the Army, the Junker. He smiles sadly: he is protected by another's lady.

* * *

A day's ride with the Army. Curses, colours, laughter—the countryside is dazzling with them. Motley-clad boys come running. Brawling and calling. Girls come with crimson hats in their flying hair. Beckoning. Soldiers come black-armoured, abroad like the night. Seize the girls hotly, tearing their clothes. Press them against the drum's edge. And under the fiercer resistance of quick hands the drums come to life, as in a dream they rumble, rumble. And in the evening they offer him lanterns, strange lanterns: wine shining in iron casques. Wine? Or blood? Who can tell?

* * *

At last before Spork. The Count towers beside his white steed. His long hair has the glint of iron. Von Langenau has asked nothing. He recognizes the General, leaps from his charger, and bows in a cloud of dust. He brings a letter of recommendation to the Count. But the Count commands: "Read me the scrawl." And his lips have not moved. He does not use them for that; they are all right for swearing. Anything more than that his right hand says for him. That's all. And you can see that it

does. The young man has finished long ago. He does not know
now where he is. Spork fills the scene. Even the sky has withdrawn. Then Spork, the great general, says: "Cornet."
And that is much.

✣ ✣ ✣

The company lies on the far side of the Raab. Von Langenau
rides over there, alone. A plain. Evening. The metal on the
front of his saddle shines through the dust. And then the moon
rises. He sees this from his hands.
He is dreaming.
But then something shrieks at him.
Shrieks, shrieks,
Rends his dream.
That is no owl. Merciful Heaven:
The solitary tree
shrieks at him:
Man!
And he looks: something rises writhing. A body rises
writhing against the tree, and a young woman,
bleeding and bare,
assails him: set me free!

And he leaps down into the green blackness
and severs the hot thongs;
and he sees her eyes glow
and her teeth gnash.
Is she laughing?
Horror grips him.
And already he is in the saddle,
Galloping into the night. Bloodstained cords fast in his hand.

✣ ✣ ✣

Van Langenau is writing a letter, deep in thought. Slowly he
limns out in great, solemn, upright letters:

"Dearest Mother,
"be proud: I carry the flag,
"be undisturbed: I carry the flag,
"love me: I carry the flag——"

Then he puts the letter in his tunic, in the most secret place, beside the rose petal. And thinks: It will soon be scented by it. And thinks: Perhaps some one will find it some day. . . . And thinks: . . . for the enemy is near.

✻ ✻ ✻

They ride over a slain peasant. His eyes are wide open, reflecting something, but not the heavens. Later, dogs howl. So a village is near, at last. And above the cottages stonily rises a castle. The broad bridge comes to meet them. The gateway stands wide. High-pitched the horn's welcome. Listen: Rumbling, rattling, and baying of dogs. Whinnying in the courtyard, noise of hooves and of voices.

✻ ✻ ✻

Rest! To be a guest for once. Not always to meet one's own desires with scant fare. Not always to lay enemy hands on things; for once to let everything happen and to know: what happens, is good. Courage, too, must take its ease for once and come to rest at the touch of silken coverlets. Not always to be a soldier. For once to wear flowing locks and a wide open collar and to sit in silken seats and to feel to the very finger-tips the well-being after the bath. And to learn afresh what women are. And how the white ones behave and what the blue ones are; what their hands are like, the way their laughter sings, when fair-haired boys bring lovely dishes laden with luscious fruits.

✻ ✻ ✻

It began as a meal. Then it became a feast, one hardly knows how. The tall flames flickered, the voices thrilled, a medley of song broke from the glass and the gleaming, and at last, from the perfected rhythms, came the dance. And all were carried away. The beat of its waves filled the halls, a meeting and choosing, a parting and finding again, delight in the brilliance, the blinding of lights and the swaying in the summer winds of warm women's dresses.

From darkling wine and thousand roses the hour flows foaming into the dream of night.

✻ ✻ ✻

And there is one who stands and gazes with wonder upon this splendour. And his is such a nature, that he waits to see if he will waken. For only in sleep is such splendour seen, such festivals of such women: their smallest gesture is the falling of a fold in brocade. They raise up hours of silver speech, and ofttimes lift their hands up so—that you must think, somewhere, beyond your reach, they pluck fair roses, which you cannot see. And then you dream: Of being adorned with them and knowing other happiness and winning a crown for your brow, which is bare.

✻ ✻ ✻

One, who wears white silk, knows that he cannot wake; for he is awake and perplexed by present things. And so, in fear, he flees into a dream and stands in the park, alone in the dark park. And the feast is far off. And the light lies. And the night is close about him and cool. And he asks a woman, who bends to him:

"Are you the night?"

She smiles.

And then he feels ashamed of his white dress.

And would fain be far away, and alone and in armour.

In full armour.

✻ ✻ ✻

"Have you forgotten that you are my page for this day? Would you leave me? Where are you going? Your white dress gives me a right to you——"

. . . .

"Are you longing for your rough coat?"

. . . .

"Are you cold? Are you homesick?"
The Countess smiles.
No. But that is only because his childhood state, that soft dark robe, has fallen from his shoulders. Who has taken it away? "You?" he asks in a voice he has not heard before. "You!"
And now he has no covering. And he is naked as a saint. Shining and slender.

✶ ✶ ✶

Slowly the castle lights go out. All are weary: with labour or love or are drunk. After so many endless, empty nights at the front: beds. Broad oaken beds. Here prayers are different from those in the wretched trench on the march, which becomes like a grave as one falls asleep.
"Lord God, as Thou willest!"
These prayers in bed are shorter.
But more deeply felt.

✶ ✶ ✶

The turret-chamber is dark.
But they shine into each other's faces with their smiling. They grope with their hands like the blind, each finding the other like a door. Almost like children afraid of the night, they cling close to each other. And yet they are not afraid. There is nothing there that is hostile to them: no yesterday, no to-morrow; for time has perished. And they blossom forth from its ruins.
He does not ask: "Your husband?"
She does not ask: "Your name?"
They have, indeed, found each other, to be each to each a

new generation. They will give each other a hundred new names and take them all off again, gently, as one takes off an ear-ring.

✽ ✽ ✽

In the antechamber von Langenau's tunic, his bandolier and his mantle hang over a chair. His gauntlets lie on the floor. His flag stands upright, leaning against the window's cróssbar. It is black and slender. Without, a storm sweeps across the sky, tearing the night into pieces, white and black. The moonlight passes like a long flash of lightning; and the motionless flag has restless shadows. It is dreaming.

✽ ✽ ✽

Was a window open? Is the storm in the house? Who is slamming the doors? Who is passing through the rooms? Let be. Whoever it is. He will not find his way to the turret chamber. As if behind a hundred doors in this deep sleep, which two people share; share like *one* mother or *one* death.

✽ ✽ ✽

Is that the morning? What sun is rising? How big is the sun? Are those birds? Their voices are everywhere.
Everything is bright, but it is not day.
Everything is full of sound, but it is not the voices of birds.
It is the beams that blaze. It is the windows that scream.
And they scream, red, into the midst of the enemy, lying out there in the flickering landscape, scream: Fire.
And with fragments of sleep in their faces, all crowd, half in armour, half naked, from room to room, from passage to passage, and seek the stairs.
And with muffled breath the bugles stutter in the courtyard: Fall in, Fall in!
And throbbing drums.

✽ ✽ ✽

But the flag is not there.
Shouts: Cornet!
Plunging horses, prayers, shouting.
Curses: Cornet!
Iron against iron, command and bugle-call;
Silence: Cornet!
And once again: Cornet!
And away goes the galloping cavalry.

.   .   .   .

But the flag is not there.

* * *

He races to out-strip the blazing corridors, through the burning embrace of red-hot doors, down stairways that scorch him, he bursts forth from the flaming building. In his arms he is carrying the flag like a white, swooning woman. And he finds a horse, and like a shout: he is gone, over and past all before him, past his own troops. And then the flag comes again to itself, and never was it so regal; and now they all see it, far ahead, and know the bright, helmetless man and know the flag. . . .

But then it begins to shine, floats in the wind, and grows large and red. . . .

.   .   .   .

For their flag is aflame in the midst of the foe, and they dash in pursuit.

* * *

Count von Langenau is right in the midst of the enemy, but quite alone. Fear has made a round space about him, and he stands, in the midst of it, beneath his slowly consuming flag.

Slowly, lost almost in thought, he gazes about him. He sees colours and strange things before him. Gardens—he thinks and smiles. But then he feels that eyes are fixing him and sees men and knows that these are the pagan dogs: and flings his horse into their midst.

But, as they close in about him, they seem to be certainly gardens again, and the sixteen curved sabres, which leap up towards him, flash after flash, are a festival. A laughing fountain display.

* * *

The tunic was burnt in the castle, the letter and the rose-leaf of a lady unknown.—

The next spring (it came in sad and cold) a courier of the Freiherr von Pirovano rode slowly into Langenau. There he beheld an old woman weeping.

QUARTET ENCOUNTERS

The purpose of this new paperback series is to bring together influential and outstanding works of twentieth-century European literature in translation. Each title has an introduction by a distinguished contemporary writer, describing a personal or cultural 'encounter' with the text, as well as placing it within its literary and historical perspective.

Quartet Encounters will concentrate on fiction, although the overall emphasis is upon works of enduring literary merit, whether biography, travel, history or politics. The series will also preserve a balance between new and older works, between new translations and reprints of notable existing translations. Quartet Encounters provides a much-needed forum for prose translation, and makes accessible to a wide readership some of the more unjustly neglected classics of modern European literature.

Aharon Appelfeld · *The Retreat*

Translated from the Hebrew by Dalya Bilu
with an introduction by Gabriel Josipovici
'A small masterpiece . . . the vision of a remarkable poet'
New York Times Book Review

Grazia Deledda · *After the Divorce*

Translated from the Italian by Susan Ashe
with an introduction by Sheila MacLeod
'What [Deledda] does is create the passionate complex
of a primitive populace' D.H. Lawrence

Carlo Emilio Gadda · *That Awful Mess on Via Merulana*

Translated from the Italian by William Weaver
with an introduction by Italo Calvino
'One of the greatest and most original Italian novels
of our time' Alberto Moravia

Gustav Janouch · *Conversations with Kafka*

Translated from the German by Goronwy Rees
with an introduction by Hugh Haughton
'I read it and was stunned by the wealth of new material . . .
which plainly and unmistakably bore the stamp of Kafka's
genius' Max Brod

Henry de Montherlant · *The Bachelors*

Translated from the French and with an introduction
by Terence Kilmartin
'One of those carefully framed, precise and acid
studies on a small canvas in which French writers
again and again excel' V.S. Pritchett

Stanislaw Ignacy Witkiewicz · *Insatiability*

Translated from the Polish by Louis Iribarne
with an introduction by Czeslaw Milosz
'A study of decay: mad, dissonant music; erotic perversion;
. . . and complex psychopathic personalities'
Czeslaw Milosz

Hermann Broch · *The Sleepwalkers*

Translated from the German by Willa and Edwin Muir
with an introduction by Michael Tanner
'One of the greatest European novels . . .
masterful' Milan Kundera

Pär Lagerkvist · *The Dwarf*

Translated from the Swedish by Alexandra Dick
with an introduction by Quentin Crewe
'A considerable imaginative feat'
Times Literary Supplement

Robert Bresson · *Notes on the Cinematographer*

Translated from the French by Jonathan Griffin
with an introduction by J.M.G. Le Clézio
'[Bresson] is the French cinema, as Dostoyevsky
is the Russian novel and Mozart is German music'
Jean-Luc Godard, *Cahiers du Cinéma*

Rainer Maria Rilke · *Rodin and other Prose Pieces*

Translated from the German by G. Craig Houston
with an introduction by William Tucker
'[Rilke's] essay remains the outstanding interpretation
of Rodin's œuvre, anticipating and rendering otoise
almost all subsequent criticism'
William Tucker, *The Language of Sculpture*